1

THE MINISTRY OF THE CELEBRATION OF THE SACRAMENTS

VOL. I

SACRAMENTS OF INITIATION AND UNION

CELEBRATION OF BAPTISM
CELEBRATION OF CONFIRMATION
CELEBRATION OF THE EUCHARIST

VOL. II

SACRAMENTS OF RECONCILIATION

CELEBRATION OF PENANCE
CELEBRATION OF ANOINTING OF THE SICK

VOL. III

SACRAMENTS OF COMMUNITY RENEWAL

CELEBRATION OF HOLY ORDERS
CELEBRATION OF MATRIMONY

THE MINISTRY OF
THE CELEBRATION OF THE SACRAMENTS

Sacraments of Initiation and Union

Nicholas Halligan, O.P.

Volume I
Baptism, Confirmation, Eucharist

ALBA · HOUSE   NEW · YORK

NIHIL OBSTAT:
Very Rev. Joseph C. Taylor, O.P., S.T.M., Ph.D.
Very Rev. William B. Ryan, O.P., S.T.M., J.C.D.

IMPRIMI POTEST:
Very Rev. Terence Quinn, O.P., S.T.L., Provincial

NIHIL OBSTAT:
Very Rev. Joseph C. Taylor, O.P.
Censor Deputatus

IMPRIMATUR:
Patrick Cardinal O'Boyle
Archbishop of Washington
August 28, 1972

The *Nihil obstat* and *Imprimatur* are a declaration
that a book or pamphlet is considered to be free
from doctrinal or moral error. It is not implied
that those who have granted the *Nihil obstat* and
Imprimatur agree with the contents, opinions or
statements expressed.

Current Printing (last digit):

9   8   7   6   5   4   3   2   1

LIBRARY OF CONGRESS
CATALOGING IN PUBLICATION DATA

Halligan, Francis Nicholas, 1917-
Sacraments of initiation and union.

(His The ministry of the celebration of the
sacraments, v. 1)
Includes bibliographical references.
1.Baptism—Catholic Church. 2. Confirmation—
Catholic Church. 3. Lord's Supper—Catholic
Church. I. Title. II. Series.
BX2200.H25 vol. 1   [BX2205]   264'.02'008s   [265'.1]
ISBN   0-8189-0272-8   (v. 1)   73-4222
ISBN   0-8189-0271-X   (set)

DESIGNED, PRINTED AND BOUND IN THE UNITED STATES
OF AMERICA BY THE FATHERS AND BROTHERS OF THE
SOCIETY OF ST. PAUL, 2187 VICTORY BOULEVARD,
STATEN ISLAND, NEW YORK 10314 AS PART OF
THEIR COMMUNICATIONS APOSTOLATE.

Foreword

Word and sacrament in the Church of Christ are not separated but intimately united in their distinctiveness. The ministry of the word leads to the ministry of the sacraments, and the sacraments themselves are celebrated in the word. The pastoral ministry in the Church is charged with conveying to all those who respond to the invitation of the grace of Christ the unfathomable and salutary riches of both word and sacrament. The present volumes are limited to the consideration of the ministry of the sacraments and their authentic celebration.

The ministry of the sacraments is an "ad-ministration," that is, a ministering *to* the People of God. What the legitimate minister brings to them are the graces of the sacraments and the benefits of the Sacrifice of the Mass, as sacrament and sacrifice have been handed down and understood in the Church and regulated by her authority. It is a worship ministry in which the minister by ordination or deputation offers homage in the name of all. It is an authentic ministry when it is exercised in union with the bishops under the Chief Pastor and thus in accordance with and expressive of their teaching and directives.

The minister who is earnest in fulfilling his ministry with fidelity and pastoral responsibility is responsive to the guidance and direction of the Church in whose name he functions. The burden of these volumes is to provide the minister and aspirants to the ministry with authorized norms whereby they may be safely guided in practice in the ministry of the celebration of the sacraments.

Although proper theological exploration and canonical interpretation continue to exercise their helpful roles in the understanding of sacramnt and worship life in the Church, the acceptable celebration of this ministry in the pastoral care of souls has been clearly and sufficiently delineated by competent authority in the Church during the period of renewal inaugurated by the recent Council. The text of these volumes, then, as the citations indicate, proposes to make this evident from the full use of the relevant documents and pertinent directives.

The sacramental ministry is considered in the celebration first, of the sacraments of initiation and union: Baptism, Confirmation, Eucharist; second, of the sacraments of reconciliation: Penance, the Anointing of the Sick; third, of the sacraments of community renewal: Holy Orders, Matrimony.

SACRAMENTS OF INITIATION AND UNION

Foreword

Through the sacraments of Christian initiation men and women, freed from the power of darkness, who have died, been buried, and risen again with Christ, receive the spirit of filial adoption and, with the entire People of God, celebrate the memorial of the Lord's death and resurrection. Through Baptism they are incorporated into Christ, formed into God's people, and obtain forgiveness of all their sins. Raised from their natural human condition to the dignity of adopted children, they become a new creation through water and the Holy Spirit. Hence they are called, and are indeed, the children of God.

Signed with the gift of the Spirit in Confirmation, Christians more perfectly become the image of their Lord, filled with the Holy Spirit, and thus, bearing witness to him before all the world, they forthwith lead the body of Christ to its fullness.

Finally, by sharing in the eucharistic table, they eat the flesh and drink the blood of the Son of Man so that they may have eternal life and show forth the unity of God's people. By offering themselves with Christ, they share in his universal sacrifice: the entire community of the redeemed is offered to God by their high priest. They pray for a greater outpouring of the Holy Spirit so that the whole human race may be brought into the unity of God's family.

The three sacraments of Christian initiation closely combine to bring the faithful to the full stature of Christ and to enable them to carry on the mission of the entire people of God in the Church and in the world.[1]

It is through these three sacraments of initiation and unity that a man or woman officially receives identity as a Christian. As sacraments of faith, these three presuppose the gift of faith. It is faith that puts one in contact with the Lord Jesus; it is thus the effective response of each person to the Will of God, who wills that all men be saved. The sacraments incorporate the one receiving them into the Mystical Body of Christ, mature and strengthen him, and give fuller witness to that spiritual contact and incorporation; they are by institution designed to culminate in the most intimate contact and union of all in this life, which takes place in the Eucharist and which is the fulfillment, perfection, and final purpose established for all the other sacraments.

Christian life is a sacramental life. Contact with the Risen Lord Jesus is now made, although not exclusively, through the sacraments which, by positive institution of Christ, guarantee and certify, indicate and signify this contact by a seven-fold benefit conveying to men the everlasting achievement of the Passion, Death, and Resurrection of the God-made-Man.

---

1. **Ordo Baptismi Parvulorum, De Initiatione Christiana, Praenotanda Generalia,** 1-2 (S.C. pro Culto Divino, 15 maii 1969). "As members of Christ, all the faithful have been incorporated into him and made like unto him through Baptism, Confirmation, and the Eucharist. Hence all are duty-bound to cooperate in the expression and growth of his Body, so that they can bring it to fullness as swiftly as possible" (Vatican II, Decree **Ad gentes,** 36).

TABLE OF CONTENTS

THE CELEBRATION OF BAPTISM

Contents

THE MINISTRY OF THE CELEBRATION OF THE SACRAMENTS

THE CELEBRATION OF BAPTISM

I. Baptism, a Sacrament of Initiation and Unity

Baptism, from the Greek word Βαπτιζω meaning to immerse, to bathe, to wash, is a sacrament of the New Law as instituted by Christ in which, by a washing with water, performed by a right-intentioned minister invoking the Holy Trinity a wayfarer on earth is regenerated to divine and supernatural life and aggregated to the Church.[2] Of the three ways in which divine grace may be imparted for justification only Baptism of *water* is truly a sacrament actively justifying by the very fact of its proper conferral. Baptism of *desire* is the sacrament in some way truly sought for and terminating whenever possible in the actual reception of the Baptism of water; it justifies on the strength of the genuine desire. Baptism of *blood* or death suffered for the Christian faith justifies by that very event together with, in the case of adults, at least attrition.

Baptism, the door to life and to the kingdom of God, is the first sacrament of the New Law offered by Christ to all men that they might have eternal life (Jn 3:5). He entrusted this sacrament and the Gospel to his Church when he told his Apostles: "Go, make disciples of all nations, and baptize them in the name of the Father, and of the Son, and of the Holy Spirit" (Mt 28:19). Thus, Baptism is, above all, the sacrament of that faith by which all men who are enlightened by the Spirit's grace respond to the Gospel of Christ. That is why the Church believes it is her most basic and necessary duty to inspire all, catechumens, parents of children still to be baptized, and godparents, to that true and living faith by which they adhere to Christ and enter into or confirm their commitment to the new covenant. To accomplish this, the Church prescribes the pastoral instruction of catechumens, the preparation of the children's parents, the celebration of God's word, and the profession of baptismal faith.

Baptism, moreover is the sacrament by which men and women are incorporated into the Church, built into a house where God lives in the Spirit (Eph 2:22), into a royal priesthood (1 Pet 2:19) and a

2. Cf. CIC, cc. 12; 87.

holy nation. It is a sacramental bond of unity linking all who have been signed by it.[3] Because of that unchangeable effect (signified in the Latin liturgy by the anointing of the baptized person with chrism in the presence of God's people), the rite of Baptism is held in highest honor by all Christians. It may never lawfully be repeated once it has been validly celebrated, even by our fellow Christians from whom we are separated.

The cleansing with water by the power of the living Word (Eph 5:26), which Baptism is, makes us sharers in God's own life (2 Pet 1:4) and his adopted children (Rom 8:15; Gal 4:5). As proclaimed in the prayers for the blessing of the water, Baptism is a laver of regeneration (Tit 3:5) as sons of God and of birth on high. The invocation of the Trinity over those who are to be baptized has this effect that those who are signed in this name are consecrated to the Trinity and enter into fellowship with the Father, the Son, and the Holy Spirit. They are prepared for this high dignity and led to it by the scriptural readings, the prayer of the community, and the threefold professsion of faith.

Far superior to the purifications of the Old Law, Baptism produces all these effects by the power of the mystery of the Lord's passion and resurrection. Those who are baptized are engrafted in the likeness of Christ's death (Rom 6:4-5), buried with him in death (*ibid.*), given life again with him, and with him rise again (Eph 2:6). For Baptism recalls and effects the paschal mystery itself, because by means of it men and women pass from death of sin into life. Its celebration, therefore, should reflect the joy of the resurrection, especially when it takes place during the Easter Vigil or on a Sunday.[4]

By the sacrament of Baptism, whenever it is properly conferred in the way the Lord determined, and received with the appropriate dispositions of soul, a man becomes truly incorporated into the crucified and glorified Christ and is reborn to a sharing of the divine life, as the Apostle says: "For you were buried together with him in Baptism, and in him also rose again through faith in the working of God who raised him from the dead" (Col 2:12; cf. Rom 6:4). Bap-

---

3. Vatican II, Decree **Unitatis redintegratio,** 22.
4. **Ordo Baptismi Parvulorum,** 3-6.

tism, therefore, constitutes a sacramental bond of unity linking all who have been reborn by means of it. But Baptism, of itself, is only a beginning, a point of departure, for it is wholly directed toward the acquiring of the fullness of life in Christ. Baptism is thus oriented toward a complete profession of faith, a complete incorporation into the system of salvation such as Christ himself wills it to be, and finally, toward a complete participation in Eucharistic communion.[5]

By his power he is present in the sacraments, so that when a man baptizes it is really Christ himself who baptizes.[6] Thus, by Baptism, men are plunged into the paschal mystery of Christ; they die with him, are buried with him, and rise with him (cf. Rom 6:4; Eph 2:6; Col 3:1; 2 Tim 2:11); they receive the spirit of adoption as sons "by virtue of which we cry: Abba, Father" (Rom 8:15), and thus become those true adorers whom the Father seeks (cf. Jn 4:23).[7]

Through Baptism we are formed in the likeness of Christ: "For in one Spirit we are all baptized into one body" (1 Cor 12:13). In this sacred rite, a union with Christ's death and resurrection is both symbolized and brought about: "For we were buried with him by means of baptism unto death." And if "we have been united with him in the likeness of his death, we shall be so in the likeness of his resurrection also" (Rom 6:4-5).[8]

Incorporated into the Church through Baptism, the faithful are consecrated by the baptismal character to the exercise of the cult of the Christian religion. Reborn as sons of God, they must confess before men the faith which they have received from God through the Church.[9]

In Baptism neophytes receive forgiveness of sins, adoption as sons of God, and the character of Christ, by which they are made members of the Church and for the first time become sharers in the priesthood of their Savior.[10]

Baptism is called *solemn* when it is celebrated with all the rites

5. **Unitatis redintegratio, loc. cit.**
6. Vatican II, Const. **Sacrosanctum Concilium,** 7.
7. **Ibid.,** 6.
8. Vatican II, **Lumen gentium,** 7.
9. **Ibid.,** 11.
10. Paul VI, Const. **Divinae consortes naturae,** 15 aug. 1971.

and ceremonies prescribed in the liturgical books,[11] even if one
or another rite or ceremony is lacking. The mere fact that all the
ceremonies of *solemn* Baptism cannot be observed does not automatically permit the conferral of private Baptism.[12] However, the
present liturgy of Baptism provides several solemn rites to suit
the circumstances.[13] Baptism, whether for one child, or for several,
or even for a larger number, should be celebrated by the ordinary
minister and with the full rite when there is no immediate danger
of death.[14]

Baptism which is not solemn is considered to be *private*, even
if one or another rite or ceremony is employed, e.g., in imminent
danger of death.[15] Baptism conferred at home and outside of necessity by priests with a special faculty is considered to be solemn
and is to be performed with baptismal water and with all the ceremonies.[16] Except in case of danger of death, Baptism should not
be celebrated in private houses.[17]

II. Requirements for the Celebration of Baptism

A. *Requisite materials*

True and natural water is necessary for Baptism.[18] Water is
true if it is composed of the requisite elements constituting water;
natural if it is commonly considered and used as true water, whether
naturally or artificially produced, which judgment is arrived at not
simply by the results of chemical analysis but by the ordinary estimation and use of prudent men. Such true water is necessary for
the sake of the authentic sacramental symbolism. It should be clean,

11. c. 737, 2.
12. S. Off. 28 feb. 1663; 15 sept. 1869.
13. Cf. IX, below.
14. **Ordo Baptismi Parvulorum, Praenot.,** 15.
15. **Ibid.,** 21.
16. S.C.Sac. 23 dec. 1912.
17. **Ordo Baptismi Parvulorum, loc. cit.,** 12.
18. c. 737; cf. Denz.-Schön. 1615.

for reasons of health. The baptismal font, or the vessel in which on occasion the water is prepared for the celebration of the sacrament in the sanctuary, should be very clean and attractive. If the climate requires, provision should be made for the water to be heated beforehand.[19]

The following are accepted as *certainly valid material* for the celebration of Baptism: natural water in a liquid state as found in rivers, the sea, wells, springs, fountains, pools, cisterns, baths, swamps, lakes, melted snow or ice or hail, mineral water, sulphur water, dew, condensed vapors, water from sweating walls, water mixed with a small amount of an extraneous element, as in the case of muddy water, as long as the water predominates, putrid water if it still remains true water in common estimation.[20] As an antiseptic measure, one thousandth part of bichloride of mercury or some comparable antiseptic may be added to the baptismal water, e.g., in the necessary case of uterine Baptism.[21]

Materials are considered *doubtfully valid* when their substances do not certainly imply natural water or their mixture with other elements almost supplants the water. Such doubtful materials are: light tea and coffee, thin soup and broth, light beer, thin ink, water produced from salt or lye or soapsuds, artificial water extracted by distillation from flowers (e.g., rose water) or herbs or flowing from vines or trees or other plants (but all these materials are considered invalid materials by some). In every case of prudent doubt in the concrete situation the resolution should always be in favor of the valid celebration of this so necessary sacrament.

Substances which have never been water or have been so changed as no longer to be or to be considered water are *certainly invalid material*. Such invalid materials are: wine, oil, meat or fat juice, amniotic fluid, fluids from the bodies of animals and men, milk, blood, urine, saliva, tears, sweat, thick soup or gravy, lard, grease, lacquer, shoe polish, foam, phlegm, all things not in a liquid state, water mixed with another substance which predominates and is

19. **Ordo Baptismi Parvulorum, Praenot. Gen.,** 18-20.
20. S. Off. 17 apr. 1839.
21. **Ibid.,** 21 aug. 1901.

no longer considered as apt to wash, mud, ink, thick beer or soup or coffee or tea or lye.

B. *Proper Use of the Materials*

Except in the case of necessity, the priest or deacon should use only water that has been blessed for the baptismal rite. If the consecration of the water has taken place at the Easter Vigil, the blessed water should, if possible, be kept and used throughout the Easter season to affirm more clearly the relationship between the sacrament of Baptism and the paschal mystery. Outside the Easter season, it is desirable that the water be blessed for each celebration, in order that the words of blessing may clearly express the mystery of salvation which the Church recalls and proclaims. If the baptistry is supplied with flowing water, the blessing will be given to the water as it flows.[22] Thus only baptismal water is *lawfully* used, and this applies also when Baptism is celebrated outside a church or public oratory, e.g., at home.[23] It is commonly considered to be a serious requirement.

Water which has been corrupted, run out or spilled, or become foul, or otherwise is lacking should not be used. New water should be poured into the previously fully cleaned font and blessed using the formula in the baptismal rite.[24]

In a case of necessity, such as the danger of death, if certainly valid material is lacking or unavailable, doubtfully valid material can and must be used, even with the least probability of its validity (i.e., any material about which there is not certain validity). The use in this instance is conditional: "if this material is valid." The one so baptized is later to be baptized conditionally with certainly

22. **Ordo Baptismi Parvulorum, loc. cit.,** 21.
23. S.C.P.F. 8 sept. 1869. If during any season of the year the quantity of baptismal water that pastoral considerations have judged should be kept on hand runs low that there seems hardly enough, a lesser amount of unblessed water may be mixed with it, even more than once, but each time in a quantity less than the blessed water on hand (c. 757, 2; cf. S. Off. 17 apr. 1839).
24. Cf. c. 757.

valid material: "if you are not baptized." In private Baptism conferred in a case of necessity unconsecrated water is lawfully used,
although holy water is to be preferred (not under obligation) to
simply water; a priest or deacon should use baptismal water.[25]
Without great inconvenience missionaries are to consecrate water
for Baptism or have such water always at hand.[26]

Either the rite of immersion (dipping), which is more suitable
as a symbol of participation in the death and resurrection of Christ,
or the rite of infusion (pouring) may lawfully be used in the celebration of Baptism.[27] There must be in the common estimation of
men a true washing or ablution, a flowing of water whereby the
whole body or the head is washed. A *triple pouring* is made corresponding with the pronouncement of each name of the Trinity,
as in the rite. This is probably a serious obligation, even though
it pertains only to the lawful conferral of Baptism. The pouring is
made *on the head*, since the head is the principal part where life
integrally resides. Baptism is less certainly valid as the parts washed
are less noble than the head. One baptized in a case of necessity
on other than the head should be baptized conditionally at a later
time, if possible.

For the validity of a true washing the water should *flow*, even
though there be only some drops (merely one or two drops are
doubtfully sufficient). Merely to anoint the person to be baptized,
e.g., with the thumb moistened with blessed water, is not sufficient.[28]
To draw a wet cloth or sponge or wet fingers across the head or
forehead is at least doubtfully valid. The water used should flow
into the sacrarium or drainage part of the baptismal font and not
into the blessed water that is being conserved: if a font is not
employed, the water should be poured into a sacrarium or into the
ground.

The water that flows must *touch the skin*, otherwise the Baptism
is invalid or at least doubtful and thus is to be conferred again

25. S. Off. 20 iun. 1883.
26. S.C.F.P. 8 sept. 1869.
27. **Ordo Baptismi Parvul., loc. cit.,** 22. Aspersion or sprinkling is
    no longer used. (c. 758)
28. S. Off. 8 nov. 1770; 9 iul. 1779; 14 dec. 1789.

conditionally, e.g., if the water touches only the hair, (the hair should be parted to allow the water to flow on the skin, or across the forehead or tempels), or only the clothes of the one being baptized. However, Baptism is valid even if the head is covered with sores. (It is invalid if given on the body of the mother of an unborn child to be baptized, highly doubtful when given on the umbilical cord or on one of the two membranes immediately surrounding the fetus in the womb, even though they arise from the fetus. The third membrane which surrounds the fetus exteriorly is from the mother and thus Baptism on it would be invalid.)

C. Required Words

The words by which Baptism is conferred in the Latin Church are: "I baptize you in the name of the Father, and of the Son, and of the Holy Spirit."[29] This is the prescribed and *lawful* formula. In judging the *validity* of any other formula which may be used, either intentionally or otherwise, it is absolutely necessary that the following elements be present in the formula: the *minister* or the one baptizing must be expressed, at least implicitly; the *act* of baptizing expressed, in order that the pouring of the water might have significance; the *person baptized* mentioned, since the action is directed to this party; the *unity* of the divine essence, provided for by the words "in the name of"; the *trinity* of Persons, expressed by distinct and also probably by proper names.

The words of the formula are to be pronounced at the same time as the water is poured. Thus, not only moral but also physical simultaneity should be sought, since in practice the safer opinion must be followed.[30]

No one can baptize himself.[31] When someone other than the minister pours the water and the latter pronounces the form or when several ministers partially and severally cooperate in the essential part of the rite, the administration is invalid.[32] In the

---

29. **Ordo Baptismi Parvul., loc. cit., 23.**
30. Sd. Off. 4 mart. 1679; cf. Denz.-Schön. 2101. Cf. E below.
31. Innocent III, 28 aug. 1206, cf. Denz.-Schön. 788.
32. **Cf. S.C. Sac. 17 nov. 1916.**

case of immersion it is not sufficient that the one to be baptized immerse himself; the minister must lead him into the water or out of it while the baptismal formula is being pronounced. On the other hand, when a person is held by a minister under flowing water—fountain, gutter, rain—the Baptism is valid if the proper formula is used. Likewise, when someone other than the minister pours the water but the latter with his hand or with some instrument directs the water upon the person to be baptized.

Baptism may be celebrated in either the Latin language or in the vernacular in accordance with the approval Ritual.[33]

D. *Time and Place of Celebration*

The *private* celebration of Baptism, in the case of necessity, may take place at any time and in any place.[34] Those in danger of death are to be baptized without delay.[35]

1. *For children*

In the *solemn* celebration of Baptism the first consideration is the welfare of the child, that it may not be deprived of the benefit of the sacrament; then the health of the mother must be considered, so that, as far as possible, she too may be present. Then, as long as they do not interfere with the greater good of the child, there are pastoral considerations or needs, such as allowing sufficient time to prepare the parents and for suitably planning the actual celebration to bring out its paschal character.

As soon as possible and even before the child is born, the parents should be in touch with the parish priest concerning the Baptism, so that proper preparation may be made for the celebration. *An infant should be baptized within the first weeks after birth.*[36] The Conference of Bishops may, for sufficiently serious pastoral reasons, determine a longer interval of the time between birth and Baptism.

When the parents are not yet prepared to profess the faith or

---

33. **Sacrosanctum Concilium,** 36; 63.
34. c. 771.
35. **Ordo Paptismi Parvul., Praenot.,** 8.
36. **Cf. c. 770.**

to undertake the duty of bringing up their children as Christians, it is for the pastor, keeping in mind whatever regulations may have been laid down by the Episcopal Conference, to determine the time for the Baptism of infants.[37]

Although Baptism may be solemnly celebrated on any day,[38] to bring out the paschal character of Baptism, it is recommended that the sacrament be celebrated during the Easter Vigil or on Sunday, when the Church commemorates the Lord's resurrection. On Sunday, Baptism may be celebrated even during Mass, so that the entire community may be present and the necessary relationship between Baptism and the Eucharist may be clearly seen, but this should not be done too often.[39]

So that Baptism may clearly appear as the sacrament of the Church's faith and of admittance into the People of God, it should normally be celebrated in the parish church, which must have a baptismal font.[40] For a justifying reason the local Ordinary may permit the celebration to take place in the sacristy.[41] The Bishop, after consulting the local parish priest, may permit or direct that a baptismal font be placed in another church or public oratory within the parish boundaries. On these places, too, it is the normal right of the pastor to celebrate Baptism.[42]

Except in danger of death, Baptism should not be celebrated in private houses.[43] *Solemn* Baptism may never be administered in the homes of non-Catholics, not even in case of necessity or danger of death.[44] This is a serious precept. The law permits two exceptions: children or grandchildren of those holding actual supreme civil authority or those having the right of succession to the throne may be baptized in a private home upon due request.[45] The local Ordinary may prudently judge that for a just and reasonable cause

37. **Ordo Baptismi Parvul.,** loc. cit., 8.
38. c. 772.
39. **Ordo Baptismi Parvul.,** loc. cit., 9.
40. **Ibid.,** 10; cf. cc. 773; 774, 1.
41. S.C. Rit. 14 mart. 1861.
42. **Ordo Baptismi Parvul.** loc., cit., 11; cf. cc. 774, 2; 739, 1.
43. **Ibid.,** 12; cf. c. 776, 1.
44. S.C.R. 17 ian. 1914.
45. c. 776, 1, 1o; 2.

Baptism should be celebrated at home in some extraordinary case,[46] e.g., the father refuses to allow Baptism in the church, or a sick person cannot be brought to the church.[47] In such cases Baptism is to be solemnly celebrated in the chapel of the house or some other decent place and baptismal water used.[48]

Unless the Bishop decides otherwise, Baptism should not be celebrated in hospitals, except in cases of emergency or for some other pastoral reason of a pressing kind. Care should always be taken that the parish priest is notified and that the parents are suitably prepared beforehand.[49] Thus, hospital chaplains are not ordinary ministers of solemn Baptism, and children born in a hospital should be solemnly baptized by the pastor of the parents. Even when inconvenience or delay exists, the local pastor has the right. Moreover, the chapel of the hospital is only a semipublic oratory, unless the local Ordinary formally approves it as a public oratory over and above its approval as a chapel. Thus it seems that the chaplain who wishes to baptize solemnly in a hospital must obtain permission of the proper pastor of the one to be baptized, of the pastor of the parish in which the hospital is located, and of the local Ordinary who may permit it for a just and reasonable cause in an extraordinary case.[50]

If the one to be baptized cannot come or be brought, without serious inconvenience or danger, to the parochial church or to another which enjoys the right to a font, because of the distance or other circumstances, solemn celebration can and ought to be conferred by the pastor in the nearest church or public oratory within the limits of his parish, even though they should lack a font.[51] There is no need for the pastor to consult the Ordinary, but under the required conditions he may proceed under the common law. If even this exceptional procedure cannot be followed, it seems that Baptism will have to be deferred until such time as the party

46. Ibid., 1, 2o.
47. S.C. Sac. 22 iul. 1925.
48. c. 776, 2.
49. Ordo Baptismi Parvul., loc. cit., 13.
50. cc. 738; 776, 1, 2o.
51. c. 775.

can be brought to the church or until permission can be obtained from the local Ordinary to have a solemn celebration at home or other place.

2. For adults or youths of catechetical age

Since the initiation of Christians is the first sacramental participation in the death and resurrection of Christ, and since moreover the time of purification and illumination customarily falls within the Lenten season[52] and the "mystagogia" within the Paschal season, the whole initiation should thus exhibit a paschal character. And so Lent should keep its full import for a greater preparation of the elect, and the paschal Vigil itself should be considered the lawful time for the sacraments of initiation.[53] Yet it is not forbidden for these sacraments, on account of pastoral needs, to be celebrated outside these times.[54]

The celebration of Baptism of adults may take place in stages or by steps, *as established and regulated by the local Ordinary.*[55] Thus pastors ought so to use the order of initiation that the sacraments are celebrated on the paschal Vigil and the election made on the first Sunday of Lent. The remaining rites are distributed in view of this arrangement. Yet, for more serious pastoral needs, the curriculum of the whole rite may be otherwise arranged.[56]

Because of unusual circumstances and pastoral needs it is allowed that the rites of election and of the time of purification and illumination be celebrated outside Lent and the sacraments themselves outside the Vigil or the day of Easter. In even ordinary circumstances, and then only for grave pastoral needs, e.g., where very many are to be baptized, it is permitted to select, outside the curriculum of initiation customarily performed in Lent, another time, especially Paschaltide, for celebrating the sacraments of initiation. In these cases, with the moments of insertion in the liturgical

52. **Sacrosanctum Concilium,** 109.
53. c. 710 is here derogated.
54. **Ordo initiationis christianae adultorum,** 8 (S.C. pro Culto Divino, 6 ian. 1972).
55. **Ibid.,** 44.
56. **Ibid.,** 49.

year changed, the structure itself of the entire rite, with opportune intervals, should remain the same.[57] Accommodations should be made in that the sacraments of initiation, insofar as it can be done, should be celebrated on Sunday, using, as the opportunity presents itself, the Sunday Mass or a proper ritual Mass. The rite for making catechumens will take place at a fitting time. The "election" is celebrated some six weeks before the sacraments of initiation so that enough time is had for the *scrutinia* and *traditiones*. The "scrutinia" are not to be celebrated on solemnities but on Sundays or even within the week with the customary intervals.[58]

If the simpler rite of initiation is used, the celebration should take place, insofar as can be done, on Sunday with the actual participation of the local community.[59]

The rites should be carried out in befitting places, as indicated in the Ritual. There should be consideration of the peculiar needs which arise in secondary stations of mission regions.[60]

E. *Excursus: Union of the requisite material and the prescribed formula in the Sacraments.*

1. *Norm*

The requisite material of a sacrament is some sensible, concrete material thing to be used (as water poured in Baptism) or sensible action to be employed (as the acts of the penitent expressed in Penance) in the confection or celebration of a sacrament.

The prescribed formula of a sacrament is the words or some other equivalent signs (as a nod expressing consent in Matrimony) which determine or perfect the significance of the required matter in particular, both thus constituting the external sign and producing the sacramental effect. In order to qualify for a sensible sign, the formula must be pronounced vocally (or equivalently, as is possible in Matrimony) and not mentally only.

The required material and prescribed formula in each sacra-

57. **Ibid.,** 58.
58. **Ibid.,** 59-63.
59. **Ibid.,** 244.
60. **Ibid.,** 63.

ment must be united by the minister in such a way that they can be truly said to constitute the one sign instituted by Christ. Thus some union of the material and the formula is required for *validity* at least, in order that the words of the formula be verified, with the type of union varying for the different sacraments. Union is either *physical*, if the words of the formula are pronounced at the same instant the matter is applied (to say "I baptize you..." and at the very same time to pour the water), or *moral*, if the material and the formula are successively applied (to say "I baptize you..." and subsequently to pour the water).

For the *Eucharist* a physical conjunction of both the material and formula being pronounced is always absolutely required. The pronoun "this" (*hoc* and *hic*) in the formulas of consecration is not verified unless the material it designates is physically present to the minister. It is common teaching that for the validity of *Baptism, Confirmation, Anointing of the Sick, Holy Orders* a moral conjunction will suffice. The application of the requisite material may be made immediately before or immediately after the formula is pronounced without the words of the formula losing their meaning or verification. Whether any delay (such as less time than it takes to say an *Our Father*) between the application of the material and the pronunciation of the formula invalidates the sacrament is controverted. However, wider latitude in moral union is recognized for *Penance* and *Matrimony*. Since Penance is administered after the manner of a judgment and Matrimony follows the nature of a contract, the penitential judgment may be extended over a notable period of time before being completed, and the matrimonial consent of one party may be supplied later to validate the contract, as long as the consent of the other party perseveres.

The *lawfulness* of sacramental administration requires that the minister observe that union of the two elements prescribed by the Church in her rites.[61] *In the case of the sacraments it is regularly unlawful to use a merely probable opinion at the risk of nullity of the administration.*[62] Thus, in practice, the physical union as

61. c. 733, 1.
62. Innocent XI (S. Off. 4 mart. 1679) condemned the proposition: "It is not unlawful in the conferral of the sacraments to

prescribed by the rubrics, especially in Baptism, Confirmation, Anointing of the Sick, is to be observed, whatever the theoretical opinion, and even though the sacrament would have to be repeated conditionally.[63] Care should always be taken that the requisite material and the prescribed formula are so united that at least one has begun before the other is finished.

With the exception of Penance and Matrimony (by reason of their character of judgment and of contract) the application of the material and formula of each sacrament must be conjoined by one and the same minister on the same subject of conferral.[64] This is demanded by the signification of the words of the formula. However, many ministers applying the whole material and pronouncing the entire formula at the same time validly confect a sacrament, e.g., many ministers baptizing at the same time the same infant, the formula must be pronounced simultaneously by all. In the Latin Church multiple ministers of a sacrament are usually permitted only in the concelebration of the Eucharist and in the conferral of the episcopal character. If a sacrament is made up of many parts, e.g., in the Eucharist, Anointing of the Sick, many ministers validly act, each administering a part, as long as each minister places that part of the material corresponding to the formula he pronounces. Thus the signification of the words of the formula is verified if one minister using the prescribed formula anoints the forehead, another the hands. This is gravely unlawful, except in the case prescribed by the Church when the celebrant of Mass dies immediately after the consecration of the bread.[65]

2. *Alteration*

In the administration of the sacraments by fallible ministers

follow a probable opinion regarding the validity of a sacrament, while abandoning a safer one" (Denz.-Schön. 2101).

---

63. S. Off. 2 maii 1858, to the Vicar Apostolic of Abyssinia, commanded that Baptism be repeated conditionally whenever the formula is pronounced after the water has been poured or vice versa.
64. S.C. Sac. 17 nov. 1916.
65. Cf. **Missale Romanum** (older editions), **de Defectibus, X.** 3.

it sometimes occurs that the requisite material is not rightly applied or the prescribed formula altered, due to inadvertence, negligence, error, or deliberate will. In any case the objective change that results will be either substantial or accidental. Judgment of the quality of the change affected will be made not by the criteria of the physical sciences but in accordance with the common usage and estimation of prudent man.

A *substantial* change takes place when in ordinary usage and prudent estimation the material no longer remains of the same species and name as that determined in the sacrament (e.g., to use milk in baptizing), or when the words used in the formula no longer retain the same sense (e.g., to say "I restore you . . ."). A change is *accidental* when the material remains the same in usage and name but altered in some accidental quality (e.g., to use leavened bread or a square host), or when the words of the formula are different but retain the same sense (e.g., to say "I wash you . . ."). However, if the corrupt formula cannot have other than a sacramental sense, it generally remains a valid formula. Thus the separation of individual words or of syllables does not constitute a substantial alteration, unless the interval is long enough to alter the meaning of the sentence (more easily admissible when syllables are separated). In such a case the moral unity of the formula as one complete prayer is destroyed by the interruption and also by such grammatical changes or mistakes as could actually change the meaning of the formula. Substantial alteration may also be risked by faulty articulation or by clipping words through haste. In practice where a complete word is actually interrupted through a pause between syllables, it is advisable to repeat the word, unless the interruption is extremely slight.

A *substantial* change of material and formula always invalidates a sacrament, whereas a *purely accidental* change does not have this effect. It is never permitted and it is always gravely sinful to use a substantially altered material or formula in the sacraments; it is a sin of irreverence to the sacrament, uncharity to the recipient who is thus deprived of a sacramental benefit, injustice on the part of a minister who has by office the care of souls. The use of an accidentally altered element outside of grave (and not always extreme) necessity is sinful, because it violates reverence for the sacrament and contravenes the precept of the Church.[66] It is slightly or seriously sinful depending upon the degree of voluntary alteration, but clearly seriously sinful when attributable to contempt or to a deliberate will to introduce a new rite of administration. When some grave necessity urges, such an administration may be lawful, e.g., when only non-consecrated water is available in the case of an urgent Baptism.

3. *Use of a condition in doubt*

Since the occasion for using a doubtful formula would very rarely arise, the principles pertinent to the use of doubtful material would apply equally in the case of a doubtful formula. Doubtful material is that which is not certainly apt for the valid conferral of a sacrament, e.g., tea in Baptism. It is never lawful, but rather it is seriously sinful to use doubtful material when certain material is available, since nullity of the sacrament is risked without sufficient reason; likewise, charity and justice may also be violated. In defect of certainly valid material urgent and grave necessity will permit the use of doubtful material. The administration must be conditional, e.g., "If this is valid material. . . ." The conditional administration thus retains due reverence for the sacrament, and the possibility of the sacrament being validly administered provides for the spiritual necessity of the recipient. The necessity will be determined by the nature of each sacrament, e.g., Baptism, Penance and sometimes Anointing of the Sick are necessary for salvation, whereas the Eucharist is not so necessary and the danger of idolatry in the use of doubtful material here can never be tolerated.

The formula prescribed by the Church for each sacrament is absolute, i.e., its truth does not depend upon any condition or circumstance. However, in some cases a *conditional formula* alone will be possible. The condition ought to be—and regularly is presumed to be—with respect to *validity* of the sacrament and not its lawful conferral or reception or fruitfulness.[67] The condition may be

---

66. c. 733.
67. Cf. c. 732, 2.

of the past, e.g., "if you have not been baptized...," or of the present, e.g., "if you are alive..." or of the future, e.g., "if you will have restored...." Excepting the case of the sacrament of Matrimony, a conditional formula in the sacraments is valid only when the condition is of the past or the present. In such situations, if the condition of the formula is verified, the material and the formula being thereby conjoined, the sacrament is valid; a future condition would impede any physical or moral conjunction of the necessary elements and thus invalidate the administration. Matrimony, following the nature of a contract, can be validly entered into under a future condition. It will take its effect at the future verification of the condition, as long as the consent of both parties perseveres.

No sacrament may be administered under a condition without a just cause, because of the danger of nullity and irreverence. As in the case of doubtful material, grave urgency may require a conditional administration where absolute administration is impossible due to a doubt about the material or of the previous administration or of the capacity of the recipient, e.g., with the unconscious. Outside of such necessity as the salvation of the recipient, a just cause will permit but it does not oblige a conditional administration. The justifying cause will vary with different sacraments. To act without sufficient cause would be seriously sinful, but only slightly sinful if the minister is morally certain the condition is verified. The justifying cause may be founded upon *charity*, e.g., if the confessor does not recall imparting absolution to a worthy penitent, or *justice*, e.g., if a sacerdotal ordination is prudently doubted, or *religion*, e.g., if the celebrant prudently doubts having pronounced the words of consecration at Mass. As a general rule, a sacrament may be conferred conditionally when there is danger of it being invalid if administered absolutely, or when a person would be deprived of a great good or his salvation imperilled if the sacrament were denied absolutely.

In every sacramental administration the condition must be expressed *at least mentally*, as the circumstance enters into the very intention of the minister. In practice, it is advisable to express every condition orally in words, in order to assure the placing of the condition. It is controverted whether the intention to administer a sacrament as it should be administered according to the mind of the Church includes implicitly and virtually each necessary condition; or whether this is too generic and indefinite, especially in those instances when the law and the Ritual state very precise conditions, as otherwise there would be no particular point in especially prescribing conditional administration. In any case, the purpose of a condition is not to assure validity but to prevent the serious irreverence of administering a sacrament invalidly when all the requisites for validity are not present.

III. Minister of Celebration

A. *Solemn celebration*

The ordinary minister is he who in virtue of his *power of Orders* is deputed primarily to confer solemn Baptism. The ordinary ministers of Baptism are Bishops, presbyters, and deacons. At every celebration of this sacrament they act in the Church in the name of Christ and by the power of the Holy Spirit. Thus it is incumbent upon them to be diligent in the ministry of the word of God and in the celebration of the sacraments, avoiding any action which the faithful can rightly condemn as favoritism.[68]

Bishops, who are the principal dispensers of the mysteries of God and leaders of the entire liturgical life in the church committed to them, direct the conferral of Baptism, by which a sharing in the kingly priesthood of Christ is granted. For this reason they should personally celebrate Baptism, especially at the Easter Vigil. In a special way the preparation and Baptism of adults is commended to their care.[69]

It is the pastor's duty to assist the Bishop in the instruction and Baptism of the adults entrusted to his care, unless the Bishop

---

68. **Ordo Baptismi Parvul., Praenot. Gen.,** 11.
69. **Ibid.,** 12; cf. c. 744.

makes other provisions. It is also his duty, aided by catechists or other qualified lay people, to prepare and help the parents and godparents of children with appropriate pastoral guidance and then to administer Baptism to the children.[70]

1. *Proper pastor*

The celebration of Baptism pertains *by reason of office* to the proper pastor (and local Ordinary)[71] of the one to be baptized. It is a reserved function, a parochial right or pastoral act, since by Baptism one is aggregated to a particular church or parish and thus is to be received by the one who enjoys jurisdiction in the church. Where parishes or quasi-parishes are not yet established (as in some missions), the particular statutes and accepted customs must be consulted to determine which priests, besides the Ordinary, have the right to baptize, either in the entire territory or in some particular district.[72]

A parish priest or pastor (*parochus*) *by title* is a priest or moral person to whom is entrusted a parish with the care of souls to be exercised under the authority of the local Ordinary.[72a] This is the pastor in the proper or strict sense, possessing the parish *in titulum* or in his own right. His is the right and duty to preach and to administer the sacraments to a specific body of the faithful who are thereby constituted the proper recipients of his ministry.

A priest who merely administers a parish, and thus does not possess it in his own right but rather *in administrationem*, is placed in the same category as a pastor with all the rights and duties of the same[73] including the celebration of Baptism, e.g., a quasi-pastor and some parochial vicars.[74]

---

70. **Ibid.,** 13.
71. c. 198.
72. c. 740.
72a c. 451. 1.
73. **Ibid.,** 2.
74. 1. **quasi-pastor.** This is the priest (**quasi-parochus**) in charge of a subdivision of a vicariate or prefecture in mission territory (cc. 451, 2, 1o; 216, 3).
    2. **parochial vicar.** He enjoys the rights and duties of a pastor, if he possesses full parochial powers (c. 451, 2, 2o).

The *lawful* administration of Baptism is not reserved to any pastor but only to the proper pastor of the one to be baptized. The proper pastor is he in whose parish a person establishes domicile or quasi-domicile;[75] if the same person has a plurality of domiciles or quasi-domiciles, the several pastors have equal rights. The above also applies to the rite of bringing a baptized child to the church when necessity has justified a previous private celebration. A merely conditional Baptism without ceremonies does not seem to be a parochial right. The proper pastor of a convert is in practice

a) **vicar of a moral person.** He has the actual care of souls in a parish which is attached to a moral person, e.g., a religious community, which is considered to be the habitual possessor of the parish. He is designated as **vicarius actualis** or **vicarius curatus** and enjoys full parochial powers (c. 471).

b) **vicar econome.** Usually called in the U.S.A. the administrator of the parish (**vicarius oeconomus**), he is appointed to care for a vacant parish pending the appointment of a new pastor. In this category falls the priest who takes charge until an administrator is appointed, e.g., the first assistant, the neighboring pastor, or the religious superior (c. 472). The administrator enjoys full parochial powers (c. 473).

c) **substitute vicar.** When the pastor is to be away for more than a week, a priest to take his place (**vicarius substitutus**) is to be appointed by the pastor with the approval of the local Ordinary or by the latter. He enjoys full powers unless some restrictions have been imposed by the pastor or the local Ordinary (cc. 474; 465, 4-5). A substitute or **sacerdos supplens** who supplies the needs of the parish for less than a week's time is not a substitute vicar.

d) **auxiliary vicar.** When a pastor becomes unable to fulfill his duties because of old age, mental disability, blindness or other permanent affliction, the local Ordinary shall appoint a priest to take his place. Called **vicarius adjutor,** he may or may not be granted full parochial powers (c. 475).

e) **parochial assistant.** He is the curate or ordinary assistant of the pastor (**vicarius cooperator**) who is appointed by the local Ordinary to assist the pastor who, because of the number of souls or other reasons, cannot alone care for his parishioners. The extent and character of his parochial powers come from diocesan statutes, his letters of appointment by the local Ordinary, and the commission of the pastor (c. 476). He does not act in the place of the pastor but rather as his helper.

---

75. c. 94, 1.

the pastor of the place of administration. A national pastor has the right to baptize only his own national parishioners; a non-national pastor has no right to baptize nationals having their own pastor.

The right of the proper pastor to baptize is both personal and territorial. Thus he may normally baptize only his own parishioners within the limits of his own parish. For *lawful* celebration in another parish he needs the permission of the Ordinary or the pastor of that place (this applies also to a local Ordinary outside his territory).[76] Consequently, although a pastor can hear the confessions of his subjects anywhere,[77] he is restricted to his own territory in the administration of Baptism,[78] Anointing of the Sick,[79] Viaticum,[80] and Matrimony.[81] In general, pastoral functions are subject to the authority of the pastor of the place where these functions are to be performed.

2. *Parishioner*

A person is called a resident (*incola*) in the place where he has a *domicile*.[82] This latter is acquired by residence in a parish or quasi-parish, or at least in a diocese, vicariate, or prefecture apostolic,[83] provided that the residence is either combined with the intention of remaining there permanently (even though a change of residence may become desirable in the future), or is continued for ten years.[84] A minor has the domicile of the one in whose care he is; a wife not lawfully separated has that of her husband.[85]

A person is said to be a tenant (*advena*) in the place where he has a quasi-domicile.[86] This latter is acquired by residence with the intention of staying in the places mentioned above for at least

76. c. 739.
77. c. 873, 1.
78. c. 739.
79. c. 938.
80. c. 850.
81. c. 1095.
82. c. 91.
83. c. 92, 3.
84. **Ibid.,** 1.
85. c. 93, 1.
86. c. 91.

the greater part of the year, unless one is called away, or by an actual residence prolonged for the greater part of the year.[87]

A visitor or stranger (*peregrinus*) is one who is presently outside the place where he has a domicile or quasi-domicile.[88] A visitor should be baptized solemnly in his own parish by his proper pastor, if this can be done readily and without delay.[89] Parents are commonly considered to sin seriously when outside the case of necessity and without the permission of their proper pastor they bring their child to other priests to be baptized. The necessity itself need not be grave. However, if the child cannot be presented to the proper pastor readily and without delay, any pastor can solemnly baptize the visitor within his territory.[90] Typical cases would be the delicate health of the infant, the lack of transportation, the expense involved, etc. Diocesan statutes may precise more accurately in practice the extent of the impediment when a child is born outside the bounds of the parental parish.

A person is homeless or a wanderer (*vagus*) if he has neither domicile nor quasi-domicile.[91] His proper pastor or proper Ordinary is the pastor or Ordinary of the place in which he is presently staying; they have the right to baptize him solemnly.[92]

3. *Other ministers*

Other priests and deacons, since they are cooperators in the ministry of Bishops and parish priests, also prepare candidates for Baptism and, with the invitation or consent of the Bishop or parish priest, confer the sacrament.[93] It is the duty of the deacon, to the extent that he has been authorized by the local Ordinary, to administer Baptism solemnly and to supply the ceremonies which

---

87. c. 92, 2.
88. c. 91.
89. c. 738, 2.
90. **Ibid.**
91. c. 91.
92. c. 94, 2-3.
93. **Ordo Baptismi Parvul., Praenot. Gen., 14.**

may have been omitted when conferring Baptism on children and adults.[94]

Thus, he who *by right* celebrates Baptism can give permission (*licentia*) to another minister (priest or deacon) to baptize within the parochial limits under the care of the pastor granting the permission. It is not strictly delegation, since there is no power or jurisdiction actually given but merely the consent of the lawful pastor for another minister to exercise lawfully the power of his order within the pastor's parish. No cause is required that the pastor give his consent.

It is commonly taught that other ministers sin seriously who baptize outside of necessity and without ordinary or delegated faculty or permission, since they do grave injury to the right of another. However, there may be reasons excusing at least from serious sin. Another minister can baptize solemnly in the case of necessity, since the proper permission is lawfully presumed.[95] True necessity need not be one of danger of death; it may arise because the pastor is absent or impeded and the celebration would be put off for some time or neglected, or the child is ill and the proper pastor is not available, or the distance from home or hospital to the parish church is too great. Blood relationship with the one to be baptized is not sufficient cause to presume permission.

B. *Private celebration*

Observing the use of proper materials and the required words and intention, private Baptism may be validly celebrated by anyone, baptized or not.[96] In imminent danger of death and especially at the moment of death, when no priest or deacon is available, any

---

94. Motu proprio, **Sacrum Diaconatum Ordinem,** 22 (18 jun. 1967);
    Motu proprio **Ad pascendum,** 15 aug. 1972; cf. **Lumen gentium,**
    29. Pont. Comm. for interpret. of documents of Vat. II, 26 mart.
    1968 (**AAS** 1968, 363): a deacon who intends to go on to the
    priesthood has the powers contained in **Lumen gentium,** 29,
    and **Sacrum Diaconatum Ordinem,** 22.
95. c. 738, 1.
96. c. 742, 1. The rite consists solely in the application of the
    essential material with the formula (S. Off. 15 sept. 1869).

member of the faithful, indeed anyone moved by the right intention, may and sometimes must administer Baptism. If it is a question only of danger of death, then the sacrament should be administered by a member of the faithful, if possible, according to the shorter rite. Even in this case a small community should be formed to assist at the rite, or at least one or two witnesses should be present, if possible.[97] If the minister is a priest or deacon, he supplies the ceremonies which follow the actual Baptism;[98] it seems also that, if there is no danger in delay, the ceremonies before the actual Baptism should be observed. It should be noted that the *Shorter Rite* for the initiation of adults, when permitted, is a solemn and not a private celebration of Baptism.

The danger of death indicating the celebration of private Baptism need not be imminent or certain, but a probable danger or well-founded fear suffices. The latter can be more easily admitted in mission territories; moreover, where customary, catechists or well-instructed, trustworthy Christians may administer Baptism privately to infants of Catholic parents, even though the children are in good health, if the Catholic priest is absent or it is difficult to go to him.[99]

Baptism may be administered privately with permission of the local Ordinary to baptized non-Catholics who in adult age are baptized conditionally.[100] This may be in any church, unless the local Ordinary rules otherwise. The local Ordinary should see to it, in each case, what rites are to be retained and what omitted in the conditional conferral of Baptism.[101]

The sacrament of Baptism cannot be repeated, and thus it is not allowed to confer Baptism again conditionally unless there is

---

97. **Ordo Baptismi Parvul., loc. cit.,** 16.
98. c. 789, 1.
99. Cf. S.C.F.P. 10 feb. 1888; 16 ian. 1804. Infants baptized by midwives can be conditionally rebaptized in particular cases where there is **reasonable doubt** of the validity of the first Baptism (S.C. Conc. 19 dec. 1682). Likewise, infants baptized at home in case of necessity are to be rebaptized when there is **probable doubt** of the validity of the first Baptism (**ibid.,** 27 mart. 1863).
100. c. 759, 2.
101. **Ordo initiationis christianae adultorum, Appendix,** 7.

present a prudent doubt about the fact or the validity of the Baptism already conferred. If, after a serious investigation made because of a prudent doubt about the fact or validity of a Baptism already conferred, it seems necessary to confer Baptism again conditionally, the minister should opportunely explain the reasons why Baptism in this case is conferred conditionally and administer it in a private form.[102]

A certain precedence in baptizing is to be observed; a priest is to be preferred to a deacon, a deacon to an inferior cleric, a cleric to a lay person, a man to a woman, unless for the sake of decency or because she knows the required words and the manner of baptizing better a woman is to be preferred.[103] Even a suspended priest is to be preferred to others who are not priests, but a layman is preferred to a cleric who is under censure after sentence has been passed.[104] Although a priest may be available, it will always be more becoming for a physician or midwife to baptize a child before actual birth or while it is being born, if such a need should arise; a woman would be preferred to the father, if he were the only man present. It is unlawful for a mother or father to baptize their own offspring, except in danger of death, where there is no other person present who may baptize;[105] spiritual and carnal parentage would then originate with the same person.

The observance of this order or preference does not seem to be of serious obligation. If there is a question of violation of a sacerdotal right, e.g., a priest is present and willingly able to baptize, it is commonly held to be a serious sin. Likewise, if an infidel, heretic, or schismatic,[106] or one personally excommunicated is preferred without necessity to a Catholic man.

All lay persons, since they are members of a priestly people, and especially parents and, by reason of their work, catechists, obstetricians, women who are employed as family or social workers or as nurses of the sick, as well as physicians and surgeons, should

102. **Ibid.**
103. c. 742, 2.
104. S. Off. 20 lug. 1671.
105. c. 742, 3.
106. S. Off. 20 aug. 1671.

know the proper method of baptizing in cases of necessity. They should be taught by parish priests, deacons, and catechists. Bishops should provide appropriate means within their dioceses for such instruction.[107]

If possible, there should be two or at least one witness present by whom the administration of Baptism may be proved.[108] They can testify to the act of Baptism and the use of the elements required for validity. They may or may not be sponsors; one unable to act as a godparent may be witness. The pastor who judges the validity of a private Baptism should first have the one baptized narrate what was done; if this is not satisfactory, he should then interrogate the minister and the witnesses separately.

C. *Excursus: Obligations Involved in the Celebration of the Sacraments*

1. *Requisite Power*

A sacramental celebration does not depend for its *validity* on the disposition of the minister; its action has its effect from the power of Christ as the due sacramental action is performed (*ex opere operato*). It is not in itself affected by lack of faith, state of grace, or holiness on the part of the minister but only on the fact that the minister is divinely empowered according to the institution of Christ.[108a]

2. *Due attention*

The minister of a sacrament must have that *attention* without

---

107. **Ordo Baptismi Parvul., loc. cit., 17.**
108. **Ibid.,** 16; c. 742, 1.
108a. Cf. Denz.-Schön. 1612; 1617. Vatican II, Decree **Presbyterorum Ordinis,** 5: "God, who alone is holy and bestows holiness, willed to raise up for himself as companions and helpers men who would humbly dedicate themselves to the work of sanctification. Hence, through the ministry of the Bishop, God consecrates priests so that they can share by a special title in the priesthood of Christ. Thus, in performing sacred functions they can act as the ministers of him who in the liturgy continually exercises his priestly office on our behalf by the action of the Spirit."

which the administration would not be a truly human action. Attention is the application of the mind to what is being done; it is an act of the intellect (intention is of the will), and is opposed to distraction. Since man cannot always act with full or actual advertence but is sometimes distracted even involuntarily, it is necessary and sufficient to be truly human and responsible that his action proceed in some way from a deliberate will. An *internal attention,* i.e., which is free from all voluntary distraction, is not necessary, since Christ did not intend to require of the minister of his sacraments a condition which at times would be impossible. For a *valid* celebration the minister must have at least *external attention,* i.c., that deliberateness which is responsible for and the cause of the external action of the sacramental rite and which excludes any action physically incompatible with internal attention (if the latter were present or suddenly required). Thus, external attention is the "follow through" resulting from the minister's intention to administer the sacrament, although he is distracted at the time by surrounding circumstances or by thoughts of things other than what he is doing. Lack of external attention implicitly revokes the intention to administer a sacrament and thus invalidates it.

A lawful celebration requires also *internal attention,* which excludes all voluntary distraction. This degree of reverence for the sacredness of the sacramental rite is to be expected from one who is Christ's minister in this action of conferral of grace. A voluntary distraction is usually a slight sin; it may be serious if danger is present of substantial error in the sacramental action, e.g., through carelessness or hastiness in the use of the required material or in the pronunciation of the customary formula. Attention, therefore, answers the question: how much must the individual be aware of what he is doing; intention responds to the query: what must the individual will to do and how must he will it.

3. *Sufficient intention.*

The valid celebration of a sacrament demands of the minister a *right intention.* Intention is an act of the will by which a person resolves to do something or to omit something. Being a human or animated instrument of Christ and in order that his action might be therefore intelligent, the minister must will to use his power in conformity with the disposition of the principal agent, Christ. Thus, for a valid sacrament the minister must have a true and serious intention,[109] not only to perform an external rite but also a sacramental rite, i.e., he must have an internal intention.[110] He thereby wills to do through the means of the sacramental sign that which the Church does. His intention determines what this required material and this formula shall signify sacramentally.

In regard to the quality of intention on the part of the minister placing the action, his *intention* is *actual*, (*volitum actualiter*), i.e., his will or intention is being elicited here and now while the sacramental action is in progress, e.g., his intention to administer the Anointing of the Sick at the time he is anointing. Or *virtual*, (*volitum virtualiter*), i.e., his intention was made or elicited at a previous time and never retracted but in some way is now influencing the sacramental action being performed here and now; he is doing what he is now doing precisely because at some time previously he had determined or intended to do it, e.g., having intended to say Mass the priest prepares for and celebrates it but in a distracted manner. Or *habitual* (*volitum habitualiter*), i.e., his intention was made at some previous time and not revoked but here and now it does not exert any positive influence on the action he is performing (it may be said to have negative influence in the sense of not having been retracted and thus remaining as it were in a condition of habit), e.g., a minister baptizing while very intoxicated, insane, or hypnotized. Thus the previously elicited intention, although remaining habitually, because not retracted, is not the reason for and the cause of the action being performed at the moment. (An habitual intention is a disposition to receive but not to act.)

An habitual intention is called: *explicit*, if what was intended

---

109. Cf. Denz.-Schön. 1611.
110. Alexander VIII (S. Off. 7 dec. 1690) condemned the proposition: "Baptism is valid when conferred by a minister who observes the entire external rite and the form of baptizing, while he resolves within his own heart: I do not intend what the Church does" (Denz.-Schön. 2328).

was clearly and distinctly apprehended, e.g., a dying unconscious Christian who, when well, expressed by word or sign his desire to receive the last sacraments in danger of death and never later retracted this will is said to have such an intention to receive the sacraments; *implicit*, if what was intended was not clearly and distinctly apprehended but in some way contained in the object explicitly known and willed, e.g., the same dying person who never evidenced this desire when well or ill but yet lived as a Christian or at least never abandoned his religion.[111] Or *interpretative*, i.e., a will or intention which has never been elicited either explicitly or implicitly and does not exist presently, yet it is considered that the individual would have elicited it if he had thought of it or could think of it; as a matter of fact there is no real intention at all but merely a hypothetical one, e.g., an intention of receiving Baptism in an unconscious infidel who has been leading a naturally good life and who knows nothing of Baptism: he would want to be baptized if he knew what it was and meant. The interpretative intention is, in a sense, based upon a presumption of the future, that if the person were to know, he would intend the object. A habitual implicit intention is based upon a presumption of a presently existing (although not active) intention as perceived from some fact or disposition in the past.

An *actual* intention in the administration of a sacrament is always highly desirable and more secure, if not always within the power of the minister. A *virtual* intention suffices for the validity of a sacrament, since it alone (and never an habitual or interpretative intention) positively influences the sacramental action of the minister and causes the union of the required material and the prescribed formula to signify sacramentally. It is of faith[112] that the object of the minister's intention must be *to do what the Church does*. He is performing a sacred rite in the name of Christ and thus must intend what Christ, and therefore the Church of Christ, intends. It suffices that this intention be implicit, i.e., contained in his intention to do what Christ instituted or what the true Church does or what

111. Cf. c. 943.
112. Cf. Denz.-Schön. 1611.

Christians believe in or what is requested of the minister. The latter need not believe in God or in Christ, in the institution of the Church or in the Roman Church, in the sacrament or its efficacy, as long as he intends to do what actually in the Church by Christ's institution is a sacrament.

The intention of the minister must be sufficiently *determined*, i.e., definite and specific regarding the required material and the recipient of the sacrament. Thus (unless the intention is exclusive) it is sufficient to intend, for example, to absolve or to baptize the individual present, although the minister is unaware or even in error that it is a male and not a female, or to consecrate all the hosts before him, although he is unaware of or even in error regarding the exact number. If the intention of the minister is not precise and inclusive in accordance with the nature of the matter or of the recipient of the sacrament, the intention is invalid, e.g., to consecrate some hosts in a ciborium not indicating which ones, or to say "I absolve you" not distinguishing which of two individuals are to be absolved.

The intention must always be *absolute*, as a sacrament may be conferred under a condition only for proportionate cause. In a conflict of *contrary intentions* the one prevails which explicitly or implicitly revokes the other, notwithstanding the chronology of the intentions. Otherwise, if one intention succeeds another, the latter prevails, since it is actually influencing the sacramental action of the minister. If two intentions are simultaneous, the predominant one is that which would have been chosen by the minister if he had known of their repugnance. But if it cannot be so ascertained which prevails, the sacrament is null, for the impossible is intended and one intention destroys the other. In doubt of prevalence or of succession of intention, the sacrament is doubtfully valid.

4. *Freedom from sin and penalty*

The *lawfulness* of a sacramental celebration requires the minister to be free from serious sin and from ecclesiastical prohibitions, and that he be properly deputed. The role of minister of Christ in the sacraments demands by consecration and office a holiness which is at least a freedom from grave sin. The minister in serious sin must always at least elicit an act of perfect contrition and, in the case of the celebration of Mass, go to confession beforehand, if a confessor is available.[113]

A minister *certainly sins seriously* who in the state of serious sin fulfills three simultaneously concurring conditions: 1) he is ordained for the sacrament conferred, 2) he confects or celebrates the sacrament (which coincides with its administration in every sacrament except the Eucharist), 3) he does so solemnly (outside of necessity and with the rites and ceremonies prescribed by the Church). Lacking any of the conditions the minister will certainly sin but not always seriously. To celebrate a sacrament without necessary and proper permission or legitimate presumption, outside of necessity, is unlawful and sinful, being a violation of another's right.

5. *Duty to celebrate*

The obligation of a minister in the celebration or administration of a sacrament[114] will be qualified by his status, the condition of the petitioner, and the necessity of the request. Ministers of the sacraments are either those who have the care of souls or those not so entrusted. *Ministers with the care of souls* are: local Ordinaries, pastors or their equivalent by law or institution, canonically instituted curates, military chaplains, hospital or prison or community chaplains, clerical religious superiors. Their obligations toward that part of Christ's flock entrusted to their care urge in *justice*, from the quasi contract entered into on assuming the office or delegation (clerical religious superiors are probably bound in religion or obedience). *Ministers not having the care of souls* are bound to celebrate or administer the sacraments out of *charity*, lest their neighbor be deprived of a needed spiritual good which has been entrusted to the minister requested.

A *reasonable request* for the celebration or administration of a sacrament is made: 1) in *common need* or *light necessity*, such as the need to satisfy an obligation to receive the sacrament, e.g.,

113. c. 807.
114. c. 682.

during Paschal time, or to overcome serious sin or to withstand grave temptation which may otherwise be overcome only with difficulty and for which the grace of the sacrament is desired, or out of devotion for spiritual progress. 2) in *serious need* when only with notable difficulty would the petitioner without the sacrament be able to save his soul, although absolutely he could, e.g., a dying inveterate sinner who has perhaps forgotten how to make an act of contrition or who finds it very difficult. 3) in *quasi extreme need*, when the petitioner can scarcely otherwise save his soul, e.g., an infidel or heretic in danger of death, a dying sinner who cannot elicit an act of perfect contrition. 4) in *extreme need*, when salvation can be obtained in no other way, e.g., dying unbaptized children or unconscious adult sinners.

The obligation of the minister in each case will be affected by the necessity of the sacrament requested. Thus where the minister is called upon to risk his life, his obligations involve certainly only the absolutely necessary sacraments, viz., Baptism, Penance, and Anointing of the Sick in default of Penance. The minister is also befittingly prepared to celebrate or administer the non-necessary sacraments. A pastor or other minister may also be relieved of his obligation inasmuch as he uses a substitute (unless he is requested by name), or inasmuch as he is impeded or other ministers are readily at hand. For a minister, especially one with the care of souls, to be bound to celebrate or administer a sacrament with the concurrent proximate, very grave, and certain risk of losing his own life there must be a moral certainty of the proportionate need of the recipient *and* a morally certain hope of a successful administration, with no greater evils following upon the fulfillment of this obligation (such as the loss of a pastor depriving many other needy of a shepherd, as in mission countries), e.g., it is improbable that the dying person can be reached before succumbing or before the minister loses his own life.

Therefore, in the celebration or administration of the sacraments: 1) in *common need, pastors of souls* are held even with serious inconvenience but not at the risk of their life;[115] *non-pastors*

115. Cf. c. 467; **Rit. Rom.,** tit. I, no. 5.

are, outside of necessity, generally held lightly and without any inconvenience. Thus a pastor sins seriously who refuses even once a serious request made because of an obligation or necessity of receiving a sacrament, or frequently refuses requests made solely from devotion, or whose denial brings injury to the reputation of or great anxiety to the one requesting, or who harms souls by persistently showing his displeasure or irritation and by his tardiness, or who seldom provides Mass or confession for his people. A refusal now and again is not a serious sin, unless the sacrament is necessary, since there is no grave injury or neglect of duty. For a sacrament that is not necessary the minister, every time he is requested, would not be bound to grave inconvenience, such as to travel at a great distance, in bad weather, while indisposed. He would not sin at all if the request was unreasonable or indiscreet (e.g., at an unsuitable time) or inordinate (e.g., repeated out of scrupulosity). The minister is perhaps also excused in putting off the celebration or administration until a more suitable time, without inconvenience to the petitioner. 2) in *grave need, pastors of souls* are held at the risk of their own life to administer Baptism and Penance[116] and also the Eucharist and Anointing of the Sick when possible. *Non-pastors* are bound with grave if not notable inconvenience, but not at the risk of their own life. 3) in *extreme* or *quasi extreme need, both pastors and non-pastors* are bound even at the risk of their own life.[117]

The Church requires that the celebration or administration of the sacraments be gratuitous. However, offerings spontaneously given on the occasion or regulated by a provincial council of bishops or by legitimate custom may be accepted.[118]

6. Refusal to celebrate

The sacraments must be refused those who are incapable and those who are unworthy of them, since the sacraments require certain conditions and dispositions for their reception as befitting their

---

116. S.C.C. 12 oct. 1576.
117. cc. 892; 939.
118. cc. 736; 1507, 1; cf. **Presbyterorum Ordinis, 20.**

nature and the action of Christ in them.[119] A sacrament must be
denied to one *incapable* of receiving it, since the celebration or
administration would be invalid, a simulation, gravely sacrilegious
and intrinsically evil, e.g., to baptize an unwilling adult, to absolve
an infidel, to ordain a woman. This is never lawful, even to avoid
the loss of life.

A sacrament is to be denied to one who, although capable, is
unworthy to receive it due to sin. The holy things of God should
not be given to the indisposed.[120] Fidelity to his office as minister
of Christ, charity toward his neighbor lest he cooperate in another's
sacrilege, and the avoidance of scandal to the faithful gravely oblige
the minister to refuse his administration or celebration. The minister
should make himself morally certain of the worthiness of the recipient, which must be positively evidenced in the case of the
Baptism of adults, Penance, Orders, and matrimonial impediments;
otherwise a presumption of worthiness suffices in the absence of
evidence to the contrary.

A sacrament may be *lawfully* celebrated or administered to the
unworthy only for a *very grave reason*, all scandal being removed.
Such cooperation in another's sin of sacrilege is permitted only
for proportionate cause, lest greater evils result from a refusal (but
never when a sacrament is asked for out of hatred of the faith or
contempt of religion, which would be intrinsically evil). In practice,
an excusing reason would be: 1) to avoid violation of the sacramental seal; 2) to avoid grave scandal arising or causing the faithful
to be disturbed so that, not knowing the cause of the refusal, they
are led to stay away from the sacraments fearing lest they also
may be repulsed; 3) to avoid defaming an occult sinner, with
consequent general damage to all, or probably even without this
damage;[121] 4) to avoid very serious private injury to the minister,
such as death or some morally equivalent evil.

Thus the celebration or administration of a sacrament, especially the Eucharist, to a public or an occult sinner, who seeks it

119. Cf. IV C below.
120. Mt. 7:6; c. 855.
121. **Summa Theol.**, III, q. 80, a. 6, ad 2.

either publicly or occultly (i.e., privately), will follow certain norms.[122] In regard to this, according to canon 2197 a *crime* is: 1) *public*, if it is already divulged or is so situated that it may and must be safely concluded that it will easily become commonly known; 2) *notorious in law*, after a sentence of a competent judge definitively determining the issue or after judicial confession of the delinquent made in accordance with canon 1750; 3) *notorious in fact*, if it is publicly known and if it has been committed in such circumstances that it is entirely impossible to conceal it or to offer any legal justification for it; 4) *occult*, if it is not public; materially occult if the crime itself is not known, formally occult if its imputability is not known. It should be added also that what is public in one place may be occult in another and that a public crime may later become occult. It is divulged when a notable part of the community knows the fact and the delinquent's responsibility. A crime may remain occult, even when the several persons who may know it will not spread this knowledge, but it may be public if the few who may know it are likely to divulge it. A sinner is a public sinner, absolutely speaking, who is notorious; he is a public sinner, relatively speaking, who is known as such by those who observe him asking for a sacrament. Thus:

A *public sinner* asking for a sacrament either *publicly or privately* is to be refused. Since there is no excusing cause, an administration would scandalize the faithful. (No sinner, however, is to be kept from Penance when seriously and properly disposed, or from Anointing of the Sick when unconscious.) It is more than probable that where the crime is known by most present but not by all, so that the unworthiness is not absolutely public, the sacrament is not to be denied, as the sinner retains his good name with those unaware of his crime. But if it is absolutely public, refusal is in order, even though some present are unaware of the unworthiness. Also, if the crime is unknown in the place but is public elsewhere, and unless it is foreseen that it will be divulged soon, the sacrament may be given, since no scandal will ensue. If the unworthiness is

122. **Ibid.,** corp.; cf. c. 855. Communist Party members and supporters are included (S. Off. 1 iul. 1949; 28 iul. 1950).

due to the crime only *and* does *not* require satisfaction, reparation, or the removal of scandal, it suffices that the sinner go to confession—since this can become easily known—and thereby be able to receive the other sacraments. In doubt whether the crime is public, the sacrament is to be given; if it is public, but there is doubt about the sinner's amendment, retraction, or removal of scandal, it is to be deferred. However, the prudent judgment of the moment will condition the action to be taken.

An *occult sinner* (known to the priest outside of confession) asking *privately* for a sacrament is to be *refused*. Reverence for the sacrament, charity toward one's neighbor, and absence of hardship from the denial would require the refusal.

An *occult sinner* asking publicly for a sacrament is *not* to be *refused*, as long as serious loss of his good name, grave scandal or disturbance would result from the refusal. Holy Orders is excepted,[123] since the public good demands that the unworthy be barred.

Priests with the care of souls have no obligation in *justice* toward non-catholics, but only to baptized Catholics; non-Catholics are clearly recommended to their care.[125] However, they do have an obligation in *charity* when non-Catholics are in spiritual necessity and can be aided. Non-Catholics should be encouraged to elicit the necessary acts and to retract their errors and then in charity the sacraments may be given to them; in case of doubt they should be further urged, but the doubt remaining there seems to be no clear obligation binding the minister. The Church normally forbids the administration of the sacraments to baptized non-Catholics outside the danger of death. The attitude and practice of the Church is stated in the *Ecumenical Directory* (esp. nn. 29-50; 55). In danger of death unconscious baptized non-Catholics may be absolved and anointed conditionally, if it can be surmised that they are in good faith and implicitly reject their errors, providing scandal is not

123. c. 970.
124. c. 1350. **Unitatis redintegratio,** 5: "Concern for restoring unity pertains to the whole Church, faithful and clergy alike. It extends to everyone, according to the capacity of each." Cf. also Vatican II, Declaration **Nostra Aetate;** Secr. ad unitatem Christianorum fovendam, 14 maii 1967, **Directorium.**

present.[126] A minister who unlawfully confers the sacraments is liable
to ecclesiastical penalties including suspension.[127] He must be very
discreet in his refusal of the sacraments, especially publicly, lest
those of ill will attempt to prosecute him in civil law for defamation.

7. *Simulation and pretence of celebration*

To *simulate* or feign a sacrament is for a minister to change
secretly and unlawfully either the required material or the valid
formula, or to change or withdraw the necessary intention, so that
the sacrament becomes invalid with the recipient and others being
lead into error. A rite or action (which appears to be sacramental)
is falsely placed so that externally it is signified that a sacrament
is celebrated, confected or administered, and thus the recipient
and others are deceived, e.g., to use grape juice in place of wine
at the consecration, to omit an essential word in the formula of
absolution or last anointing. Simulation is formal or material as
the concealment is intended or permitted. Simulation is *never lawful*
under any circumstances, in order to avoid an unworthy reception,
to save one's life, or for any reasons whatsoever.[128] It is a grave
and sacrilegious lie. Moreover, it is never permitted to give a
communicant an unconsecrated host, since it will be at least material
idolatry (at least for others), even though he knows it lacks consecration: it is not a simulation of sacramental confection but of
administration.

To *dissimulate* or to pretend to celebrate or administer a sacrament is to place a non-sacramental rite or action in circumstances
in which others (and *not the recipient*) falsely judge that a sacrament
is conferred. The minister intends to hide not the sacrament but the
denial or non-conferral of the sacrament. No injury is done to the
sacrament, since true or valid material and formula are not employed; there is no lie inasmuch as the bystanders have no right
to such knowledge, e.g., in place of absolution to say some prayers

---

126. S. Off. 17 mai 1916 ad 2; 1 nov. 1942.
127. c. 2364.
128. Innocent XI condemned the proposition: "Urgent grave fear
     is a just reason for simulation of the sacraments" (Denz.-
     Schön. 2129).

and to give a blessing to a penitent who cannot be absolved, or under grave fear to dissimulate refusal of consent in matrimony. The intention is not to deceive others but to hide the truth from them. This deception is lawful for a just cause which is urgent and grave, such as to avoid scandal and infamy.

8. *Repetition of celebration*

To celebrate or confer anew a sacrament already received will depend upon the validity of the previous celebration or conferral and the nature of the sacrament. Sacraments which imprint a character, when it is *certain* that they have been *validly* celebrated or conferred, may *not* without serious sin and sacrilege be readministered in whole or in part to the same subject; likewise, the Anointing of the Sick during the same unchanged danger of death and Matrimony while the same bond exists. Such repetition would be useless and a grave irreverence. Penance may always be repeated, even several times on the same day, as prudence may indicate. The Eucharist of its nature may be repeatedly administered but by ecclesiastical law not more than once on the same day to the same person, except in the cases provided in liturgical prescriptions.

In a *doubt* of the *validity* of a sacramental celebration or conferral, every sacrament *may* be repeated *conditionally*, and certain ones *must* be repeated. However, the doubt must be prudent and reasonable, since an imprudent and rash doubt causes an irreverence to the sacrament; a condition placed in such doubt is considered as not placed, and thus the repetition becomes absolute. All the sacraments may be repeated conditionally lest their fruit be lost to the recipient. Judgment whether a non-necessary sacrament ought to be readministered or celebrated again will be made on the strength of the doubt of its validity, its degree of usefulness to the recipient, and the amount of inconvenience to the minister who is to repeat it. Certain necessary sacraments must be repeated lest grave damage to religion or neighbor result: Baptism, absolution for those dying in mortal sin, Anointing of the Sick for the unconscious moribund, Holy Orders, the consecration of doubtful consecrated hosts.[129]

129. c. 938.

If there is prudent doubt that a penitent has presented *necessary* material for confession, the form can be repeated but it is not necessary, as there is no obstacle to the reception of Communion. A minister with only slight or negative doubts, such as not recalling having pronounced the words of the formula, must not repeat them, unless the contrary is positively evident or quite probable. In itself it is seriously sinful. In practice, the scrupulous are very often excused from serious sin and often from any sin, since they act either inadvertently or from a perplexed conscience, fearing to offend God if they do not repeat the form in whole or in part. They are obliged to avoid or to eradicate scrupulosity to the best of their ability.

9. *Observance of prescribed rites and ceremonies*

Rite may be said to refer to the entire legitimate manner of carrying out an act of worship, *ceremonies* to the individual actions and gestures regarding this act, although the term "ceremonies" or even "rubrics" is sometimes used for both. These ceremonies are substantial or *essential* when they regard the legitimate use of required material and prescribed formula in the sacraments, *accidental* when they regard the things instituted by the Church for their more worthy confection and administration, e.g., all those things pertaining to the solemnization of Baptism.

The greatest care and reverence must be maintained in celebrating, confecting, administering, receiving the sacraments; the rites, ceremonies, and language of the approved liturgical books must be observed; everyone must follow his own rite as approved by the Church; major clerics who fail to observe these laws are liable to suspension.[130] Thus the obligation to observe the ceremonies is

130. cc. 731, 1; 733; 1278. **Motu proprio** Paul VI, 25 ian 1964, XI: "The regulation of the sacred Liturgy depends solely on the authority of the Church: that is, it depends on this Apostolic See and, as may be provided by law, on the Bishops; and therefore no other person, not even a priest, may add, remove, or change anything in the liturgy on his own authority." Cf. **Sacrosanctum Concilium,** 22. **Rit. Rom.,** tit. I, c. un., n. 11: "When administering a sacrament, the minister will pronounce attentively, distinctly, devoutly, and in a clear voice the individual words pertaining to its form and administra-

in itself serious and binds the minister in conscience. Ceremonies which are preceptive bind lightly or seriously; those of counsel do not bind under sin, outside of contempt or scandal.

10. *Duty to safeguard the sacraments*

In the celebration or conferral of the sacraments and the consecration of the Mass it is *never* permitted to follow a merely probable opinion or to pursue a probable course of action and to abandon a safer opinion or course with regard to the *validity* of the sacraments. The validity is to be secured by the safer procedure,[131] even with non-necessary sacraments. A violation is a serious sin against *religion* by irreverence in risking nullity, against *justice* because of the tacit obligation of the pastor by his office (and more probably of any minister) to celebrate or confer the sacrament in a safe manner. Likewise, a recipient may never apply a merely probable opinion in preference to a safer one with respect to validity but only regarding the fruit or grace or effect of the sacrament, since a solid probability of the state of grace suffices for the reception of the sacraments of the living (moral certainty can be gained only by sacramental absolution, and this may involve serious inconvenience, anxieties, scruples). A probable in prefer-

tion. Likewise he will say devoutly and religiously the other orations and prayers; nor will he easily trust to his memory, which very often errs, but will recite everything from the book. Moreover, he will perform the other ceremonies and rites with such decorum and gravity of action that the bystanders will be rendered attentive and their thoughts raised to heavenly things." Paul VI, Alloc. **Vos omnes qui** to translators of liturgical books (**AAS** 57 [1965] 969-970): "It must be kept in mind that liturgical texts, approved by competent authority and confirmed by the Apostolic See, are such that they must be religiously observed. It is not allowed anyone arbitrarily (**ad suum arbitrium**) to change, diminish, amplify, omit them. . . . Those things which have been legitimately established already have the force of ecclesiastical laws, which all must obey in duty of conscience; and this all the more so when it is a matter of laws by which the holiest action of all is governed."

---

131. Cf. note 62 above.

ence to a safer opinion may be followed when the Church supplies
for a defect that may exist, e.g., in defect of jurisdiction in Penance
and Matrimony according to the terms of canon 209.

It is permitted in *urgent necessity* to follow a probable opinion
or course of action, since in the supposition a safer one is not
obtainable, e.g., to baptize or to anoint in danger of death with
doubtful material. In the conferral or reception of a sacrament
a solidly safe opinion (i.e., one which safeguards sacramental validity) may be followed, although its contrary may be safer; a safe
opinion is a morally certain one and thus more cannot be reasonably demanded, as God obliges to what is certain morally and not
metaphysically. A probable opinion may be followed, even regarding
validity or in the absence of urgent necessity or suppliance by the
Church, in the case of those who otherwise would be in a state
of perpetual anxiety of conscience, since the situation then becomes
a real and urgent necessity, e.g., a penitent who is in frequent
distress over the value of his sorrow, a celebrant who constantly
worries about his intention to consecrate, a confessor who scruples
over the dispositions of his penitents. When it is a question, not
of a valid but of a lawful celebration or administration, a probable
practical opinion may be followed, e.g., that a priest conscious of
mortal sin and who distributes the Eucharist does not commit a
grave sin.

Holy things are to be treated in a holy manner, so that *it is not
allowed rashly to expose the sacraments to nullity or unfruitfulness.*
On the other hand, *the sacraments are for men,* so that in extreme
cases it is permitted to try extreme measures. It is not allowed
to confer the sacraments on one who, it is morally certain, lacks
either the requisite intention for validity or the good disposition
of will required for their fruitful reception. In a case of extreme
necessity, when there is no positive prohibition of the Church, the
necessary sacraments may be conferred, at least conditionally, if the
lack of requisite intention and disposition is not certain and there
is at least a minimum probability of the presence of due intention
and disposition based on some single act or sign or even on the
general quality or character of the former life. In such circumstances
the law of charity to succor one's neighbor is more compelling

than the law of religion forbidding a minister to risk nullity to a sacrament. As long as there is some *probability* that the sacrament can be valid, nullity to the sacrament is to be risked than to expose a soul to the danger of eternal loss. However, there must exist *some probability* of valid reception and not *mere possibility* which is not a reasonable basis for prudent judgment and practice in moral affairs; every sacrament may be *possibly* invalid or valid.

IV. Candidates for Baptism

Every and only a human wayfarer on this earth, who is not yet baptized, is capable of receiving the sacrament of Baptism,[131a] and especially infants whose hold upon life is tenuous. Since the sacraments produce grace where no obstacle exists, it is impossible that there be an obstacle in the case of infants who need no personal disposition for a valid and lawful reception of Baptism.

In the case of Baptism, they are considered children or infants who have not yet reached the age of discernment and therefore cannot have or profess personal faith.[132] Adults are those who sufficiently enjoy the use of reason or are able to seek Baptism on their own initiative and to be admitted to it.[133]

A. *Children*

1. *Catholic parentage*

Infants are to be baptized as soon as possible; and pastors and preachers should frequently admonish the faithful of this serious obligation incumbent upon them.[134] From the earliest times the

131a c. 745, 1.
132. **Ordo Baptismi Parvulorum. Praenot., 1.**
133. cc. 745, 2, 2o; 88, 3.
134. c. 770. Cf. above II D, 1. S. Off. 18 feb. 1958, **Monitum:** "The custom has prevailed in some places of deferring the conferral of Baptism on pretended reasons of advantage or of a liturgical nature. Some opinions, lacking indeed foundation,

Church, to which the mission of preaching the gospel and of baptizing was entrusted, has baptized children as well as adults. For, in the words of Our Lord: "Unless a man is reborn in water and the Holy Spirit, he cannot enter the kingdom of God." The Church has always understood these words to mean that children should not be deprived of Baptism, because they are baptized in the faith of the Church itself, which is proclaimed for them by their parents and godparents, who represent both the local Church and the whole society of saints and believers: "The Church is at once the mother of all and the mother of each."[135]

To fulfill the true meaning of the sacrament, children must later be formed in the faith in which they have been baptized. The foundation of this formation will be the sacrament itself, which they have already received. Christian formation, which is due to children by right, seeks to lead them gradually to learn God's plan in Christ, so that they may ultimately accept for themselves the faith they have been baptized.[136]

The children of *lax* or *lapsed* Catholics, i.e., of parents who have fallen into indifferentism, who do not practice the faith without giving it up entirely, who seek the child's Baptism for social reasons, who are invalidly married, etc., may be baptized if the minister judges there is a founded hope of a Catholic upbringing as given by a member of the family, a sponsor, or by the aid of the community of the faithful. The parents should be instructed in their responsibility. If the conditions are not judged sufficient for baptizing, the parents can be invited to inscribe the child for a later Baptism, and pastoral contacts with the parents can be fostered to this purpose. Thus, rather than baptizing all such children presented and hoping for the best, or, on the other hand, tending to

> concerning the eternal lot of infants who die without Baptism, favor this delay. Wherefore, the Supreme Congregation, with the approval of the Supreme Pontiff, warns that infants are to be baptized as soon as possible according to the prescription of canon 770. It exhorts pastors, however, and preachers to urge the accomplishment of this obligation."

135. **Ordo Baptismi Parvul., Praenot., 2.**
136. **Ibid., 3.**

refuse Baptism in order not to add to the ranks of the nominal Catholics, the situation might be turned into a pastoral opportunity, perhaps with some deferral of Baptism, to bring the parents to a better appreciation of the meaning and consequences of Baptism both for themselves and for their children.[137]

In the case of a mixed marriage, the hope of Catholic education is present if the Catholic party requests the priest to baptize the child and promises to rear it as a Catholic. If possible, the non-Catholic parent should be advised of the conferral of the Baptism.[138]

The children of a Catholic parent who is dying and merely civilly married to an unbeliever should be baptized, if there is a possible hope that they might in due course be instructed in the true religion and such a promise is given; if no such hope can be entertained, administration must be denied,[139] even though Catholic godparents offer them for baptism.[140]

The *illegitimate* children born of a Catholic with a non-Catholic party may be baptized if the Catholic has control of them and asks for Baptism. Illegitimacy is not sufficient reason to refuse the sacrament, especially when Catholic education is assured. If it is foreseen that the child after Baptism will be educated outside the faith, administration is to be denied. In danger of death all the children in the above-mentioned cases may be baptized. It suffices that the danger be probable.[141]

2. Unbaptized Parentage

a. obligation

An infant of unbaptized parents can be *lawfully* baptized, even against the objection of the parents, if the danger of death of the infant is such that it is prudently judged that the child will die before it comes to the use of reason.[142]

---

137. Cf. S.C.D.F. 13 iul. 1970 (**Notitiae** 61, 69-70).
138. S.C.P.F. 29 nov. 1672.
139. S. Off. 6-8 iul, 1898.
140. **Ibid.,** 29 nov. 1764.
141. **Ibid.,** 11 ian. 1899.
142. c. 750, 1.

Provided that the Catholic education of the child is guaranteed, an infant of unbaptized parents may be *lawfully* baptized, even though in no danger of death, if the parents or guardians, or at least one of them, consent.[143] In all cases of parental unwillingness the child would be validly baptized.

b. *cautions*

Baptism is not necessary unless the child is in proximate, certain, and personal danger of death, when out of charity one *must* baptize him (at least secretly); thus the fact of a contagious disease breaking out is not sufficient cause to baptize unless the child has been affected by the disease.[144] Even in such danger of death Baptism must be omitted, if hatred of the unbaptized (especially of Mohammedans) would be aroused and even persecution of the Church incited, e.g., in mission lands; prudence demands that the benefit of one soul be sacrificed and left to God's mercy for the sake of the common welfare of the Church and of many other souls.[145] If the danger of death is only probable but not certain, Baptism *may* be administered.[146] In doubt whether the child of the unbaptized who is in danger of death and who cannot be instructed has reached the use of reason, he should be instructed as well as possible, otherwise baptized conditionally,[147] when the doubt regards his will or desire to be baptized.

Although the children of the unbaptized have a right to receive Baptism contrary to parental will, if they have reached the use of reason and are properly instructed and disposed, yet circumstances indicating impending harm to the individual or to the Christian community may advise a postponement. However, the Church does not approve of an indefinite delay in receiving Baptism, since such souls receive from the teaching and the sacraments of the Christian religion more benefit of soul and support

---

143. **Ibid.,** 2; cf. note 137 above.
144. **S.C.P.F.** 17 aug. 1777.
145. **Ibid.**
146. S. Off. 18 iul. 1894.
147. **Ibid.**

in final perseverance than from any trial of their resolve through delay of the sacrament.[148]

3. *Baptized non-Catholic and Apostate Parentages*

Baptism may be lawfully administered to infants of baptized non-Catholics, or two Catholics who have lapsed into apostasy, heresy, or schism, provided that the parents or guardians, or at least one of them, consent to the Baptism and that assurance is given that the child will be brought up in the Catholic faith.[149] Although the Church has a strict right over the children of her subjects, i.e., of all the baptized, she does not urge this right upon those so alienated from her. If the death of the child is prudently judged likely before it reaches the age of reason, it is to be baptized.[150]

It is not allowed to baptize the child if it is to remain with the apostate parents, because there is no reasonable hope (moral certainty) of a Catholic education, even if the latter offer it spontaneously.[151] If the child is brought for Baptism by both its Catholic mother and apostate father, it not being certain that the child will later be educated in the father's apostasy or superstitious practices, Baptism must be administered; if only the Catholic mother requests the Baptism, although the apostate father objects, it may be given.[152]

4. *Foundlings*

Abandoned infants or foundlings (*pueri expositi et inventi*) are to be baptized conditionally, unless after a careful investigation there is clear proof of their Baptism.[153] A tag attached to the infant attesting to the child's baptism does not suffice unless the credibility of the testifier is beyond question. Of itself the investigation must be made.[154]

---

148. S.C.P.F. iul. 1895; cf. **Ordo initiationis Christianae adultorum,** ch. V.
149. c. 751, reaffirmed by Pius XII, **motu proprio** 1 aug. 1948.
150. c. 750, 1.
151. S. Off. 29 iun. 1637.
152. **Ibid.,** 17 sept. 1671.
153. c. 749.
154. S. Off. 5 ian. 1724.

5. *Unborn and Monstrous Infants*

a. *uterine*

i. No one enclosed in the maternal womb shall be baptized as long as there is probable hope that it may be born alive and then baptized.[155] It does not befit human dignity to baptize in the womb except in case of necessity. Baptism, moreover, is a spiritual rebirth and thus normally presupposes (natural) birth. Emergency baptism of the fetus in the womb refers to a *viable fetus*, i.e., one that can live outside the womb. Theologians commonly hold that a nonviable fetus may not be baptized in the womb, since the fetal membranes may not be directly ruptured for this sole purpose as direct abortion would result, especially before the fifth month. Similarly the life of the mother may not be seriously endangered or her death hastened for the sake of this doubtfully successful spiritual benefit to the child.

ii. It is forbidden to administer a doubtful sacrament outside a case of necessity. Even in such circumstances, in uterine baptism the difficulty of procuring a certain washing of the child's head renders the administration doubtful, and it is not entirely certain that a child in the womb is a capable subject of Baptism. Consequently, the administration is conditional: *if you are capable,* or in the case, *if you are alive.* The fetus must be conditionally baptized again after birth: *if you are not already baptized,* or *if you are capable.* [156] Uterine Baptism is permitted, and is even obligatory, as soon as it is prudently judged that there is no hope of a normal birth, that the child is in real danger to its life, and that it is necessary to act promptly. (This applies also to vaginal Baptism, with due adaptations.) If the child will survive the imminent death of the mother, Baptism may be delayed until after the mother's demise.

iii. Modern improved medical techniques and instruments are available for reaching the head or some principal part of the child in the womb and washing it with water. Typical emer-

155. c. 746, 1.
156. Ibid., 5.

gency situations are: in some cases of sudden convulsions (eclampsia) or bad hemorrhages; the child will probably succumb to a difficult presentation or an abnormally protracted labor; the infant is hydrocephalous; the death of the mother is uncertain, thus preventing a cesarian section; the child will succumb before the mother dies (a skilled operator may employ a mild local anasthesia, provided the mother's demise is not hastened or caused by the desire to baptize); the child of a living mother is dying (likewise, the desire to baptize the child offers no right to take the mother's life, or to endanger or shorten it seriously). By itself the imperceptibility of the fetal heartbeat is not a sufficient sign of the necessity of a uterine administration; there must be other companion indications.

iv. Only a skilled operator, usually a physician or nurse, is expected to perform a uterine Baptism. It is necessary to provide that the cervix be dilated or incised if not readily dilatable, that the fetal membranes (amnion, chorion, and decidua) be ruptured and the amniotic fluid discharged for the water to touch and flow on the skin, that a sterile bulb syringe or other irrigating instrument filled with tepid sterile water (if time permits) be inserted as close as possible to the head so that the water is forced against the skin while the words of the formula are being pronounced. Baptism on the umbilical cord is most probably invalid.

v. In the case of a difficult or a partial delivery the necessity for baptizing urges as soon as there is concern for the life of the infant. If there is no probable hope that the child will be born normally, then if the head of the child is born and the danger of death impends, Baptism should be administered absolutely on the head; nor shall it be again baptized conditionally if the child is born alive.[157] The head is the principal part; thus, if it presents itself, the infant is considered born and the Baptism certainly valid. If a member other than the head is born, e.g., a hand or a foot, and danger threatens, that member is to be baptized conditionally (*if you are capable*); but if the child is born alive, he must be baptized again conditionally (*if you are not already baptized*, or

---

157. c. 746, 2.

if you are capable.[158] If one member appears and is baptized conditionally, and the danger of death continues while another member is born, then baptism is again conferred conditionally.

vi. Sometimes a fetus must be taken from the mother by a *cesarian section* (hysterotomy). The operation consists in the incision of the stomach and the maternal womb for the purpose of extracting the live fetus which cannot be born in the natural manner. It is unlawful if the death of the mother is quasi necessarily induced.

Theologians are not in common agreement concerning the obligation in *charity* of the living mother to undergo a cesarian section for the purpose of baptizing the child who otherwise would be deprived of this means of salvation. For this reason, as well as because all conditions permitting such an operation are not always present, and since a uterine Baptism often can be conferred, in practice a grave obligation in charity cannot be urged on the mother. Sometimes, too, a woman will consider it an extraordinary means. The operation is permitted if the fetus is viable, the mother strong enough, and the physician or operator skilled. The mother should be exhorted to undergo the operation if the birth of the child is naturally impossible, the infant in the prudent judgment of an expert (usually the physician) cannot otherwise be baptized, and if it is prudently hoped that the mother and child will be safe as a result. On the other hand, it would not seem right to say that the mother is never obliged to permit a cesarian. If she is obliged, prudence may require in the case that she be left in good faith, when it is foreseen that she may refuse and thus die in the state of sin. A physician is bound to perform the operation when requested and to exhort the patient to undergo it if necessary.

If a mother dies during pregnancy, the fetus should be extracted by those whose duty it is and, if it is certainly alive, baptized absolutely; if there is doubt as to whether it is alive, it should be baptized conditionally.[159] A grave obligation of charity requires that provision be made for the spiritual salvation of the infant

158. **Ibid.**, 3.
159. **Ibid.**, 4.

as well as the preservation of its temporal existence. A cesarian should be performed if there is moral certainty of the death of the mother, if it is probable that the fetus is living (probably after the third month and particularly if the mother's death is sudden) and viable (since otherwise it can be baptized in the womb), and a sufficiently skilled operator is available. A priest, as a rule, is forbidden to perform the operation, even on the missions, due to lack of skill, or the danger of scandal, and the obligation of decency, although he may direct others.[160] Permission must be obtained from the nearest responsible relative and all the legal precautions taken before a post-mortem cesarian operation is performed, in order to avoid incurring legal action, especially in the case of a nonviable fetus.

b. *abortive*

Abortive or premature fetuses, no matter at what stage of pregnancy they are born, are to be baptized absolutely if they are certainly alive, and conditionally if life is doubtful. Abortion is the ejection from the maternal uterus of an immature or nonviable fetus. If an abortive fetus is certainly dead, there is no Baptism; a doubtfully living fetus is baptized conditionally: *if you are alive*, or *if you are capable*. The difficulty, however, lies in determining when this product becomes an embryo or fetus, and if it is alive when aborted. It seems to be a fetus about three months after conception or when a sufficiently human form appears, in which case absolute Baptism would be conferred; prior to this the administration would be at least conditional: *if you are a man*, or *if you are capable*. Within six months after conception Baptism should be immediate because of the precarious hold on life. The usual sign of life is movement; before the end of the third month signs of life are difficult to discern. If the fetus is of normal color, it should be baptized; if there is evidence of putrefaction (color or odor), life is absent.

As it is usually small, a fetus or embryo ejected without being fully formed is best baptized by immersion. Care must be taken that

160. S. Off. 15 feb. 1780; 13 dec. 1899.

the water touches it and not merely the protective coverings. The fetus is dipped into a pan of tepid water, the enveloping membranes ruptured with finger and thumb, the amniotic fluid allowed to run out, and the whole mass moved about in the water (or warm water may be poured in the ordinary manner on a large fetus) while the words of the formula are pronounced. Movement of the water over the fetus or of the fetus in the water is essential for validity. Unless the product ejected (including the apparently stillborn) is certainly dead, it should always be at least conditionally baptized.

c. monstrous

Monsters (*monstra*) and prodigies (*ostenta*) are always to be baptized at least conditionally.[161] A monster or monstrous form of fetus is a fetus in which the appearance of a human body is totally or notably misshapen; a prodigy or unusual form of fetus is one whose members are multiplied or diminished or otherwise deformed. If there is doubt whether there is more than one human being in the birth, one is to be baptized absolutely and the others conditionally.[162]

6. Burial

A baptized fetus should be buried in consecrated ground or put back into the uterus of the dead mother and buried with her. This applies also to a stillborn child or to a dead fetus in the womb, even though unbaptized, when the mother dies. An unbaptized fetus separated from the mother should be buried in an unblessed plot close to consecrated ground. Diocesan directives or approved hospital practice are practical norms in these cases. If there is a reasonable cause present for not burying a fetus or member of the human body, these may be cremated in a manner consonant with the dignity of the deceased human body.[163]

B. Adults

161. c. 748.
162. **Ibid.**
163. NCCB, 16 nov. 1971, "Ethical and Religious Directives for Cath-

1. Norms

An adult should receive Baptism as soon as possible.[164] It is a serious sin to defer or neglect it without reasonable cause or through contempt. Culpability will be judged by the cause and the circumstances of the delay. Some deferral of the sacrament may be necessary due to the need for better instruction in the faith, or in order to avoid imminent grave evil such as the persecution of Catholics,[165] or because of fear of severe punishment or of great family animosity and even exclusion from the home, especially in the case of a minor. In any such case, the adult should immediately elicit an act of faith and of desire for the sacrament and should try as far as possible to eliminate all proximate danger of perversion. It is up to the minister, for the lawful exercise of his office, to judge prudently when the dispostions for valid and lawful reception of Baptism are present.

The rite of Christian initiation is destined for adults who, having heard the announcement of the mystery of Christ, with their heart opened by the Holy Spirit, knowingly and freely seek the living God and undertake the journey of faith and conversion. By its help and by their preparation they are strengthened by spiritual aid and at the opportune time will receive the sacraments themselves fruitfully.[166]

The rite of initiation of catechumens takes place by a certain progression or steps or threefold stage in the midst of the community of the faithful, preceded by periods of investigation and maturation: 1) when, arriving at the initial conversion, the adult wishes to become a Christian and is received by the Church as a catechumen; 2) when, having advanced in the faith and almost completed the catechumenate, he is admitted to a more ample preparation of the sacraments; 3) when, having perfected his spiritual preparation, he receives the sacraments by which he is initiated a Christian.[167]

olic Health Facilities," n. 43.
164. Cf. above II D, 2.
165. S. Off. 21 iul. 1880.
166. **Ordo initiationis Christianae adultorum,** 1.
167. **Ibid.,** 6.

The Baptism of adults is normally to be celebrated according to the rite of catechumenate by stages,[168] *once the use of the rite has been authorized by the local Ordinary.*[169] With the permission of the local Ordinary, the Simpler Rite of initiation[170] may be employed in extraordinary circumstances, when the candidate will not have been able to pass through all the steps of initiation or when the local Ordinary, in his judgment of the sincerity of the Christian conversion of the candidate and his religious maturity, decides that he may receive Baptism without delay.

In a case of proximate danger of death a catechumen or non-catechumen can be baptized with the brief rite, as long as, while not yet at the moment of death, he can hear the interrogations and respond to them.[171] If he is already received as a catechumen, he must promise that, after he has recuperated, he will finish the customary catechesis. If he is not a catechumen, he must show serious signs of conversion to Christ and of renunciation of pagan cults and not seem to be bound by obstacles to the moral life (e.g., "simultaneous" polygamy etc,) ; moreover he should promise that, after his health is restored, he will follow the whole curriculum of initiation suited to him.[172]

At the moment of death or when death is imminent and time is of the essence, the minister, omitting everything else, pours water (natural even if not blessed) upon the head of the sick person while reciting the customary formula. Provision should be made for those who have been baptized either in danger or at the moment of death, if they return to health, to be instructed by a suitable catechesis and, received into the Church at an opportune time, granted the other sacraments.[173]

2. *Unbaptized*

a. *Requisites for validity*

168. **Ibid.**
169. **Ibid.,** 2; 44.
170. **Ibid.,** ch. II.
171. **Ibid.,** ch. III.
172. **Ibid.**
173. **Ibid.,** 281-282.

An *intention* is required of adults, since they are to receive Baptism of their own knowledge and consent (*sciens et volens*).[174] Only in doubt as to the recipient's intentions or will to receive the sacrament is Baptism administered conditionally.[175] Thus an adult must have a positive will, which is at least habitual and implicit (as in the desire to become a Christian although ignorant of Baptism) of receiving Baptism, since the present order of divine providence requires that an adult be justified and saved with the accompanying consent of his own free will to this gift of God. The minimum intention may be the basis of the administration of the sacrament only in a case of danger of death, since the safer course must be followed and an explicit intention secured. A general desire to be saved is not sufficiently determined; likewise, goodness and uprightness of life are of themselves inadequate indications of sufficient intention. It is not allowed to presume a due intention of receiving Baptism in an unconscious pagan.[176]

There is a *certain obligation* binding the minister to administer conditional Baptism to an adult in danger of death and unable to ask for it, if he has given or if he gives some probable indication of his intention of receiving the sacrament; if he later recovers and doubt remains about the validity of the first Baptism, he is to be baptized again conditionally.[177] Theologians agree that some explicit desire or intention to embrace the Christian religion or the Christian way of life, even with unawareness of Baptism, implicitly contains the desire for Baptism and is a sufficient intention for its reception. It is commonly taught that even conditional Baptism may not be administered to an adult who has given no sign of intention. Some theologians teach that a dying unconscious adult, whose only evidence of intention is some expression of attrition or contrition, may be baptized, and even the unconscious moribund about whom nothing is known. Such opinions, of admittedly slight probability, are difficult to reconcile with the expressed norms of the Church

174. c. 752, 1; S. Off. 18 sept. 1850; 3 aug. 1860.
175. S. Off., **loc. cit.**
176. **Ibid.,** 30 mart. 1898.
177. c. 752, 3.

for the lawful administration of Baptism in danger of death.[178]
Although they 'may be followed on the strength of their extrinsic
authority, the minister has no certain *obligation* to baptize in such
situations.

b. *Requisites for lawfulness*

An adult shall not be baptized except after due instruction in
the faith; moreover he is to be admonished to repent his sins.[179]
But in danger of death, if he cannot be more thoroughly instructed
in the principal mysteries of the faith, it suffices for the conferral
of Baptism that he in some way manifest his assent to these mysteries and earnestly promise that he will keep the commandments
of the Christian religion.[180] Due instruction in the faith and sorrow
for sin are thus required in the adult for the lawful reception of
the sacrament of Baptism.[181]

The convert to be baptized should have a true and sincere supernatural sorrow, which is at least attrition, for all his actual, especially mortal sins. This will include a motion of hope and an implicit resolve to abandon any bad habits. Out of devotion he may
confess his previous sins, but he is not so obliged in an absolute
Baptism.[182] The unbaptized who refuses to give up sinful practices
cannot be baptized.[183]

3. *Baptized non-Catholics*

Nothing beyond what is necessary is to be imposed upon one
who, born and baptized in a separated ecclesial Community, is
received, according to the Latin rite, into full communion with the
Catholic Church.[184] In this matter the Church's practice is gov-

178. S. Off. 30 mart. 1898; c. 752, 3.
179. c. 752, 1.
180. **Ibid.,** 2. It is not enough that the recipient merely promise
    to follow instructions later upon recovery (S. Off. 30 mart.
    1898).
181. S. Off. 18 sept. 1850; 3 aug. 1860.
182. S.C.P.F. 31 maii 1823.
183. Alexander VII, 18 ian. 1658; S. Off. 10 maii 1703; 4 iun. 1851.
184. **Ordo initiationis Christianae adultorum, Appendix, 1.**

erned by two principles: that Baptism is necessary for salvation
and that it can be conferred only once.[185]

There can be no doubt cast upon the validity of Baptism as
conferred among separated Eastern Christians. It is enough therefore, to establish the fact that Baptism was administered. Since in
the Eastern Churches the sacrament of Confirmation (Chrism) is
always lawfully administered by the priest at the same time as
Baptism, it often happens that no mention is made of the Confirmation in the canonical testimony of Baptism. This does not give
grounds for doubting that the sacrament was conferred.[186] Thus,
nothing more is to be required from Eastern Christians coming
into the fullness of communion than what a simple profession of
Catholic faith requires, even if through recourse to the Apostolic
See they are permitted transferral to the Latin rite.[187]

For the admission of one baptized to full communion in the
Catholic Church there is required a doctrinal and spiritual preparation in accordance with pastoral needs adapted to each case.
The candidate should learn to adhere more and more in his heart
to the Church in which he will find the fullness of his Baptism.
During the time of this preparation some sharing or communication
in worship (*in sacris*) can take place, in accordance with the norms
of the Ecumenical Directory. An equalizing of such candidates with
catechumens is entirely to be avoided.[188]

The sacrament of Baptism cannot be repeated, and thus it is
not permitted to celebrate or confer Baptism again conditionally
unless there is present a prudent doubt about the fact or the validity
of a Baptism already celebrated or conferred. If, after serious
investigation has been made because of such a prudent doubt of
fact or validity, it seems necessary to confer Baptism again conditionally, the minister should opportunely explain the reasons why,
in this case, it is being celebrated or conferred conditionally, and
he should administer it in a private form. The local Ordinary should

185. Secr. ad unitatem Christianae fovendam, **Directorium,** 9.
186. **Ibid.,** 12.
187. **Ordo initiationis Christianae adultorum, Appendix,** 2.
188. **Ibid.,** 5.

see to it in each case what rites should be preserved and what ones omitted in a conditional conferral.[189]

It belongs to the Bishop to admit the candidate. However, the priest who is commissioned to go through with the celebration has the faculty to confirm the candidate in the rite of admission itself, unless the one to be admitted has already validly received Confirmation.[190]

4. Insane

Those who have been insane from birth or who have become so afflicted before attaining the use of reason should be baptized absolutely as infants,[191] with the rite of infants, even against parental will or knowledge, as long as there is no danger of future perversion or of scandal. If they have lucid periods and desire Baptism, they should be baptized while they have the use of reason,[192] with the Baptism of adults, being instructed and prepared as circumstances allow. In danger of death, if this desire was manifested before they became insane, they should be baptized.[193] Those suffering from coma or delirium should be baptized only when awake and willing, but in danger of death as above.[194] Deaf-mutes fall under these norms, with due regard in certain cases for modern artificial aids in the development of their mental capacity.[195]

C. Excursus: Obligations of Candidates for the Sacraments

1. For the *valid* reception of a sacrament (except Penance) neither faith nor uprightness of life is required, as the sense and practice of the Church shows in not permitting the rebaptism or reordination of heretics rightly baptized or ordained. Baptism, however, is prerequired to all the other sacraments. From the practice of the Church it is certain that no disposition or intention is re-

189. **Ibid.,** 7.
190. **Ibid.,** 8.
191. c. 754, 1.
192. **Ibid.,** 2.
193. **Ibid.,** 3.
194. **Ibid.,** 4.
195. Cf. S. Off. 4 dec. 1851; 11 dec. 1850; S.C.P.F. 17 apr. 1777.

quired of *infants* and the *perpetually insane* to receive validly the sacraments of which they are capable: Baptism, Confirmation and even Orders and the Eucharist.[196] Having no personal sin they need no personal act to be justified, and being unable to cooperate in their own salvation, the intention of Christ and the Church through the will of the minister suffices or supplies for them.

Since no *adult* is justified and saved without his own consent, the *valid* reception of a sacrament requires that he also have an *intention* of receiving it, differing in the various sacraments. It must be a positive act of the will and not a passive attitude, neither willing nor not willing, but here and now the will is said to be not obstructing rather than positively consenting; fear does not invalidate the intention, except in Matrimony by positive law. The intention must be at least *habitual* and may be *implicit*, except for Orders, Matrimony, and the Eucharist (not as Viaticum), when it must be *explicit*. However, in Penance a *virtual* intention is necessary at the time when the required material of the sacrament is placed (at least when the signs of contrition are given); in Matrimony also, since the parties are also ministers. Thus, presupposing an habitual intention, the sacraments are validly received by those who are asleep, drunk, out of their mind or unconscious. (The intentions for the individual sacraments are considered in their appropriate places.) It should be noted that *attention* is not required on the part of the recipient for validity, since a human act proceeds from the intention of the will and not from the attention of the mind, and that the sacraments enjoy the character of gifts, which do not require attention to be truly received.

2. The *lawful* and fruitful reception of the sacraments of the *living* require also the *state of grace* (known with solid probability), lest the effect of the sacrament be frustrated. A recipient in conscious serious sin commits a further grave sin; the state of grace is first to be regained normally through confession (which

---

196. Benedict XIV, Const. **Eo quamvis,** 4 maii 1745 a. 1.
197. Innocent III (1201): "He who never consents, but entirely contradicts, receives neither the effect (grace), nor the character of the sacrament" (Denz.-Schön. 781). Cf. **Prostremo mense,** Const. Benedict XIV.

is of precept for the Eucharist). To receive the sacraments of the *dead* lawfully adults need to make acts (at least implicit) of faith, hope, and at least attrition, without which acts no adult can be justified. Moreover the recipient must be free of all *censures* prohibiting reception and must observe the prescribed *ceremonies* for each sacrament.[198]

Without sufficient reason it is forbidden to *request* a sacrament for oneself or others from an unworthy minister, i.e., one who it is foreseen will sin in celebrating or conferring it. The request would be a serious or light sin in the measure of the unworthiness of the minister, of offering the occasion for another to sin, of cooperating in it and perhaps risking scandal or the danger of perversion. As long as another minister is not available and scandal is avoided, for any just reason, even reasonable devotion, it is lawful to request a sacrament from a minister who is excommunicated (excepting the sentenced and *vitandi* outside the danger of death) or suspended, and thus, a fortiori from one simply unworthy.[199] In doubt of unworthiness it is always lawful to request and to receive a sacrament. The semi-insane and the doubtfully insane are to be given every benefit of sacramental administration befitting due reverence for the sacraments.

V. Sponsors at the Celebration of Baptism

A. *Necessity and Function*

Sponsors or godparents are those who receive the one baptized from the font. Inasmuch as they take the one baptized under their care, they are spiritual parents.

It is a very ancient custom of the Church that an *adult* is not admitted to Baptism without a godparent or sponsor, a member of the Christian community who will assist him at least in the

198. cc. 2241, 1; 2250, 2; on association with Communists, cf. S. Off. 1 iul. 1949; 28 iul. 1950.
199. Cf. cc. 2261; 2284.

final preparation for Baptism and after Baptism will help him persevere in the faith and in his life as a Christian. In the Baptism of *children* also the godparent should be present to be added spiritually to the immediate family of the one to be baptized and to represent Mother Church. As occasion offers, he will be ready to help the parents bring up their child to profess the faith and to show this by living it. At least in the final rites of the catechumenate and in the actual celebration of Baptism the godparent is present either to testify to the faith of the adult candidate or, together with the parents, to profess the Church's faith, in which the child is being baptized.[200] Each child may have a godfather and a godmother, the word "godparents" (*patrini*) being used in the rite to describe both.[201]

The obligation to have a sponsor or godparent in the solemn celebration of Baptism is considered to be serious and only proportionate and reasonable causes excuse from its observance, e.g., the Baptism would have to be deferred for a long time through lack of a godparent. This obligation rests primarily upon the parents. Even in *private* celebration of Baptism a godparent is to be used if one can easily be had,[202] but this is not a serious obligation. If a sponsor was not used in the private celebration of Baptism, he is to be employed in the suppliance of the ceremonies but in this case no spiritual relationship is contracted.[203]

When Baptism is repeated *conditionally*, the same godparent, to the extent possible, is used as perhaps in the former Baptism. In the event that that same sponsor is not available, there is no need for one in a conditional administration.[204] When a Baptism is repeated conditionally, neither the godparent present at the former Baptism nor the one at the later Baptism contracts a spiritual relationship, unless the same sponsor was used for both.[205]

The candidate who asks to be admitted among the catechumens

200. **Ordo Baptismi Parvulorum Praenot. Gen.,** 8-9.
201. **Ibid., Praenot.,** n. 6; cf. c. 762, 1.
202. c. 762, 2.
203. **Ibid.**
204. c. 763, 1.
205. **Ibid.,** 2.

is accompanied by a sponsor, man or woman, who has known and helped him and is witness to his morals, faith, and will. It may happen that this sponsor will not have fulfilled the office of godparent during the times of purification, illumination, and "mystagogia." Then another is substituted for him in this role.[206]

The sponsor, however, chosen by the catechumen for his example, qualities, and friendship, delegated by the Christian community of the place and approved by the priest, accompanies the candidate on the day of election, in the celebration of the sacraments, and at the time of the "mystagogia." It is his task to exhibit in a friendly way to the catechumen the use of the Gospel in his (godparent's) own life and in his dealings with society, to help the catechumen in doubts and anxieties, to render testimony to him, and to watch over the growth of his baptismal life. Already chosen before the "election," he exercises his role publicly from the day of "election" when he gives testimony of the catechumen before the community; and his office keeps alive the moment when the neophyte, having received the sacraments, is to be helped to remain faithful to his baptismal promises.[207]

B. *Number*

In the celebration of Baptism there should be a sponsor, two at the most (a man and a woman).[208] If there is only one, it is expedient though not necessary that the sponsor be of the same sex as the candidate lest the matrimonial impediment be contracted. If, nevertheless, more sponsors are used, all contract the obligation if the conditions for validity were observed.

C. *Qualifications*

The Church has always opposed the admission to the office of sponsor or godparent of those who are unwilling to perform their obligations in this role. To guarantee the presence of the required

206. **Ordo initiationis Christianae adultorum,** 42.
207. **Ibid.,** 43; cf. also 16; 71; 104.
208. c. 763, 2; **Ordo Baptismi Parvulorum, Praenot.,** 6.

qualifications the common law indicates the conditions that pertain to the valid and to the lawful assumption of the office. In *doubt* whether one can be admitted to the valid or lawful exercise of sponsorship, a pastor shall, if time allows, consult the Ordinary[209] of the place where the Baptism is to be celebrated. If, on the other hand, the proposed sponsor is known to be unfit, the pastor must refuse to allow him to act. This should be done in a prudent and kind manner with an explanation of the laws of the Church in this matter. If the refusal will cause an extremely difficult situation, the pastor could allow the party to assist at the Baptism, thus being constituted a mere witness.

1. *Capability*

Certain qualifications are laid down for *capability* to act validly as godparent.

a. *Fundamental Requisites*

Baptism: Only those who have been validly baptized can function validly in an ecclesiastical office, such as that of baptismal sponsor.[211]

Use of Reason: Children (and the equivalent) who have not reached the use of reason cannot act as sponsors.

Intention: The sponsor should understand the nature of the obligation that is being assumed and should deliberately accept it. However, it is not necessary that the intention be to contract a spiritual relationship, as this necessarily arises as a consequence of acting as godparent. It seems that an habitual intention suffices.

b. *Status*

Because of the close communion between the Catholic Church and the separated Eastern Churches, it is permissible for a *member of one of the separated Eastern Churches* to act as godparent, together with a Catholic godparent, at the Baptism of a Catholic infant or adult, so long as there is provision for the Catholic edu-

209. c. 767.
210. c. 765.
211. c. 2256, 2o.

cation of the person being baptized and it is clear that the godparent is a suitable one. A Catholic is not forbidden to stand as godparent in an Orthodox church, if he is so invited. In this case, the duty of providing for the Christian education of the baptized person binds in the first place the godparent who belongs to the Church in which the child is baptized.[212]

However, it is not permissible for a *member of a separated community* (which is not an Orthodox community) to act as godparent in the liturgical and canonical sense at Baptism (or Confirmation). The reason is that a godparent is not merely undertaking his responsibility for the Christian education of the person baptized (or confirmed) as a relation or friend—he is also, as a representative of a community of faith, standing as sponsor for the faith of the candidate. Equally a Catholic cannot fulfill this function for a member of a separated community. However, because of the ties of blood or friendship, a Christian of another communion, since he has faith in Christ, can be admitted with a Catholic godparent as a Christian *witness* of the Baptism. In comparable circumstances a Catholic can do the same for a member of a separated community. In these cases the responsibility for the Christian education of the candidate belongs of itself to the godparent who is a member of the Church in which the candidate is baptized. Pastors should carefully explain to the faithful the evangelical and ecumenical reasons for this regulation, so that all misunderstanding of it may be prevented.[213]

C. *Kinship*

The proposed godparent may not be the father or mother or spouse of the one to be baptized (one can act as sponsor for the children of one's spouse by another marriage). It is the duty of the godparent to watch over the moral and religious upbringing of his spiritual child, when those upon whom the duty primarily

212. **Directorium,** 48.
213. **Ibid.,** 57.

rests fail. The incongruity of having both primary and secondary obligations resident in the same person is evident. Moreover, there is a certain lack of fitness in having one of the two consorts so intimately united in marriage as the spiritual parent of the other.

d. *Designation*

The one acting as godparent must have been designated by the one to be baptized or by his parents or guardians, or in the absence of these, by the minister of the sacrament. The designation is thus the prerogative of the parents, but the approval of the qualifications of the sponsor belongs to the minister. With due regard to the rite of celebration employed, the selection is made prior to the ceremony and subsequent ratification is inefficacious. If for some reason, e.g., infancy, imbecillity, the one to be baptized is unable to choose a sponsor, the parents or guardians should supply; should they fail to do so or to select one who is unqualified, the minister should supply. Where it is extremely difficult to bar an unqualified sponsor, the minister may allow him to be present as a mere *witness*.

e. *Physical Contact*

In the act of Baptism of infants it is preferred that the mother (or father) of the infant hold him.[214] Otherwise, the godparent holds the child at the time of conferral (or immediately lifts him or receives him from the baptismal font or from the hands of the minister). In the case of an *adult* the right hand of the godfather or godmother, or both, is put on the right shoulder of the one to be baptized.[215]

f. *Proxy*

For a proxy (*procurator*) to act it is necessary that he do so in the name and by the authority of some other determined person and thus his authority must be proved, i.e., certified by qualified witnesses or by a legitimate document, unless the intention of this

---

214. **Ordo Baptismi Parvulorum,** 60; 97; 124; 148.
215. **Ordo initiationis Christianae adultorum,** 220-221; 261-262.

person is known with certainty by the pastor who baptizes. The latter should know these details in order to investigate whether the designated sponsor has the requisite qualifications. Thus, one not present at a Baptism could not be said to be acting as a godparent merely on the basis that he would act if he knew of the Baptism.[216] In the absence of a very serious cause the admission of a member of a separated (non-Orthodox) community to share in the ceremonies of Baptism as proxy is gravely illicit, although valid, because the proxy assists actively in the ceremonies and may give rise to scandal. Catholics are forbidden to act as proxies for non-Catholics.[217] A parent or a spouse may validly and lawfully act as proxy for a sponsor at Baptism, although they themselves may not be the godparent in the case. Age (except that necessary for the execution of the duty) and sex are immaterial in the choice of proxy. The name of the proxy as well as that of the principal or sponsor must be entered into the baptismal register.

2. *Acceptability*

Other qualifications are prescribed for *acceptability* to act (lawfully) as godparent.[218]

a. *Age*

The one designated must have attained the fourteenth year of his age unless, in the judgment of the minister, there is a just cause for allowing a younger person, e.g., the absence of another suitable sponsor. One could act as sponsor at the commencement of the fourteenth year, i.e., immediately upon completion of the thirteenth year.

b. *Status*

The one acting as sponsor must not be excommunicated or excluded from legal acts, or infamous by law on account of a notorious delict, nor under interdict or otherwise publicly criminal,

216. S.C. Sac. 25 nov. 1925.
217. S. Off. 3 ian. 1871.
218. c. 766.

nor infamous in fact. There is no question of a sentence in these cases. Such are, e.g., the Masons,[219] militant Communists,[220] those whose life of concubinage is notorious. Drunkards, drug addicts, etc., or those who have not made their Easter duty are not excluded from sponsorship by this prohibition alone. In the terms already noted, a member of an Orthodox community may be admitted as a godparent.

c. *Knowledge*

The sponsor's knowledge of the faith should include the principal mysteries, e.g., Trinity, Incarnation, the truths in the Apostles' Creed, which knowledge can be presumed in one who is in regular attendance at church. Such knowledge must obtain in order to instruct the godchild. Inability to recite the Apostles' Creed would not seem necessarily to prevent a person from being a sponsor, since it is possible that the rudimentary truths are known but not in such a form.

d. *Religious or Cleric*

The one selected should not be a novice or a professed in a religious institute, unless there is an urgent necessity and the expressed consent of at least the local superior is obtained. Presumed permission does not suffice, even if a real need exists. One who was a religious and later left that state is not affected by this prescription. The person acting as sponsor should not be in sacred orders, unless expressed permission of his proper Ordinary is obtained. Those installed in the ministries of lector and acolyte are not excluded from sponsorship.

D. *Effects*

1. *Obligation*

The obligation of the godparent is of itself sufficiently serious. Where he is rendered incapable of exercising his office, particularly

---

219. c.2339; S. Off. 2 iul. 1878.
220. S. Off. 1 iul. 1944.

due to civil law, he is excused from the obligation. Moral impossibility of fulfillment will counterbalance the serious duty arising from the ecclesiastical precept. If the child is being raised by Catholic parents, it is presumed that the necessary instruction is being provided, unless the contrary is demonstrated.[221]

2. *Spiritual Relationship*

This is a spiritual bond which by ecclesiastical law unites certain persons by reason of Baptism. Only the minister and the godparent contract the spiritual relationship with the one baptized.[222] (No relationship arises between minister and godparent.) It does not matter whether the celebration of Baptism is private or solemn, provided it is valid. It seems that an unbaptized minister would not contract this relationship, because of his own lack of Baptism. The proxy does not contract the bond, as a true proxy is neither designated to be a sponsor nor possesses the necessary intention.[223] Strictly speaking, the minister is not excluded from being also a sponsor in the Baptism, although distinct persons are indicated. Such sponsorship is to be exercised through a proxy.[224]

VI. Stole Fee

1. Stole fees (*praestationes*)[225] are offerings given for strictly parochial functions which belong by right to the pastor, e.g., the solemn celebration of Baptism. The amount is either determined by the free will of the donor or fixed by statute or established by the custom of the place. The service may not be refused if the fee is not forthcoming. The right of the assistant priest or curate to share in the stole fee depends upon custom, diocesan statute, episcopal

221. Cf. c. 769; S.C. Sac. 25 nov. 1925.
222. 3. 768.
223. S.C. Conc. 15 mart. 1631; 13 sept. 1721.
224. S.C. Rit. 14 iun. 1873.
225. cc. 463; 1507; 2408; 2349.

decree, or the free will of the pastor. When another assists at a function that is reserved to the pastor, the latter is ordinarily entitled to the fee. Even when the pastor delegates another to act in his place, the one delegated does not thereby obtain the right to the fee, unless previously agreed upon. The pastor ought not to waive his right when for some reason, such as good will, friendship, relationship, he allows another to perform the function. In such case, when a fee is in excess of what is customary, the surplus belongs to the pastor, unless the donor clearly intends that the actual minister receive it. The donor, however, has no right over the disposition of the customary fee.

2. Although the common law does not provide for the offering of a fee specifically at Baptism, it is an almost universal custom in the Church. The fee ordinarily goes to the proper pastor as the one enjoying the right to baptize. When another baptizes in a case of necessity, the minister would not be obliged in practice to transfer the fee to the proper pastor, since the pastor's right to it in such a circumstance is not beyond question. Where a notable inconvenience arises in bringing a child to its proper church, within the first weeks after birth, the pastor of the place of actual residence may baptize and retain the fee as the proper pastor.

VII. Baptismal Register and Certification

A. *Obligation and Place of Record*

The baptismal register is the principal record among the parochial books. Every pastor has a serious obligation to note properly the reception of the sacrament of Baptism, as this is the basic document certifying one's membership in the Church and other factors relating to individual juridic status. Pastors ought carefully and without delay to inscribe in the baptismal register the names of those baptized, the minister, parents, sponsors, and the place and date of celebration.[226] It is important to write clearly and legibly,

226. cc. 777, 1; 470.

with accurate use of the index, in order to facilitate the issuance of a certificate at some future date. Some commentators even insist that the pastor himself should sign the record, even though he has delegated another to fill out the information.

Many registers have a column for the date of birth of the recipient of Baptism, but this is not strictly necessary as the record proves only the facts attending upon the administration of the sacrament. Information regarding a private celebration is to be recorded, and also the suppliance of ceremonies. The private emergency Baptism of the child of non-Catholic parentage should be inscribed in a private book and not in the regular parochial register.

The place of celebration usually need not be specified as the register itself will provide this information. However, if Baptism has been conferred in a place other than the church, e.g., a hospital, a notation to this effect should appear in the register. If Baptism has not been celebrated by the proper pastor or in his presence, the minister is to send this information as soon as possible to the recipient's proper pastor.[227] A Baptism thus celebrated or conferred outside the parish of origin is to be recorded in writing not only in the parish where it actually occurred but also in the baptismal register of the place of origin.[228] The place of origin is the place where the father has his domicile at the time of the birth of the child.[229]

B. *Particular Data*

1. *Recipient*

The name of the recipient of Baptism is the first thing to be noted. If the name of a saint, or a name of some Christian significance is added in Baptism to a previously possessed name, both names are entered into the register. The conditional Baptism of a convert is also noted; it is good practice in this case to note a marriage contracted in heresy or infidelity. It is most important also to note the rite in which the person was baptized or to which

227. c. 778.
228. S.C. Sac. 29 iun. 1941, 11 d; S.C. Conc. 31 ian. 1927.
229. Cf. c. 90, 1.

he juridically belongs, if this differs from the rite of the place of Baptism. Notice should also be sent to the proper pastor of the juridic rite of affiliation.

2. *Minister*

Inclusion of his name is especially required, as he is the principal witness to the valid celebration. Moreover, a lay person in conferring the sacrament contracts the diriment impediment to marriage of spiritual relationship. The name of the priest who assisted at the suppliance of the ceremonies should also be recorded.

3. *Sponsors*

Apart from the obligations assumed and the spiritual relationship contracted, the names of the godparents are of great importance in the event that it later becomes necessary to prove the fact or the validity of the conferral of the sacrament. When the sponsors do not contract the spiritual relationship, e.g., at the suppliance of the ceremonies, the entry is to be made in such a way as to make this clear. When a proxy is employed, both the names of the godparent and of the proxy are entered with the latter clearly indicated.

4. *Parents*

In the ordinary case the names of the parents of the one baptized are inscribed in the register, the maiden name of the mother being entered. However, certain cases arise which require an exceptional procedure. The insertion of the parents' names is controlled by the desire to avoid the loss of good reputation. Should there be difficulty in particular cases, the local Ordinary is to be consulted who will then have recourse to the Holy See.[230] All documents relating to parenthood and its certification should be posted in the register itself. It should be noted that, in the case of a marriage of conscience, the secrecy surrounding such a union demands equal caution with respect to the Baptism of any offspring. The registration is made in the special book kept in the secret archives

230. Cf. PCI 14 iul. 1922.

of the episcopal curia.[231] The child is baptized in the ordinary way but on the completion of the ceremony the pertinent facts are reported to the local Ordinary.

a. *illegitimate children*

When there is a question of illegitimate children the name of the mother must be inserted in the register if her maternity is publicly known with certainty, or if she freely requests this in writing or before two witnesses; the name of the father must also be included, provided that he willingly requests this of the pastor either in writing or before two witnesses (their names and addresses or means of location are entered into the record), or his paternity is known from an authentic public document; in other cases the child is registered as the offspring of an unknown father or of unknown parents.[232] This also protects the pastor from future libel action. The baptismal record is never to make direct and explicit mention of the fact of illegitimacy. When the name of either or of both parents of an illegitimate child are entered in the register a notation should be made in the record describing the canonical basis for the entrance. If the children have been born of adultery, incest, or sacrilege, the same procedure as above prevails in entering the parental names, but all occasion of loss of reputation must be avoided.[233]

Often the fact that an unmarried woman is the *mother* is known publicly, i.e., it has already been divulged or the circumstances are such that it can easily become known.[234] However, if her maternity is not publicly known and is unlikely to become so later, insertion of her name depends upon her permission. If she lawfully requests that her motherhood be recorded, the request must be respected.

The fact that a particular man is publicly reputed to be the *father* of an illegitimate child is not sufficient for recording his name in the register, but the conditions of law are to be observed.

231. Cf. c. 1107.
232. c. 777, 2.
233. PCI 14 iul. 1922.
234. Cf. c. 2197, 1o.

An affidavit by a man would not of itself suffice, unless there was appended to it a request that his name be so entered. The declaration of an unmarried mother is clearly unacceptable for registering a man as the father. If the real parents subsequently marry validly, the name of the father can be inserted if: (1) he signs a document acknowledging fatherhood and requesting his name be recorded; (2) the pastor making the entry has a copy of the certificate of the marriage between the parents; (3) the pastor has investigated and found that there was no diriment impediment to the marriage at the time the child was born. The last two points enable the pastor to note that legitimacy was effected by subsequent marriage.

If two Catholics (or anyone bound to the Catholic form) have failed to observe the canonical form of marriage, it should be noted that the child is the offspring of parents married only civilly (e.g., *matrimonium civile* or *matrimonium attentatum*). If at least one of the parents was in good faith regarding the marriage at the time of the child's conception, it should be noted that the marriage was putative (and thus the child is legitimate).

If the name of neither parent can be inserted in the record, the child is to be designated as born of *unknown* parents (e.g., *parentes ignoti*). If only the mother's name is recorded, the father is recorded as unknown. If the child has been born six months after the marriage of the mother or within ten months of the dissolution of the conjugal bond, it is *presumed* that conception took place during the marriage[235] (and thus the child is legitimate). This presumption stands even though the husband declares he is not the father and the mother admits to infidelity. Proof to the contrary must be brought forth and until this is done the name of the husband remains in the register as the father of the child baptized.

b. *Foundlings and Adopted Children*

In registering the Baptism of a foundling there should be included a notation of the day, the place, and by whom the child was found; also an estimate of the age of the child. In the case of a

235. c. 1115, 2.

child baptized subsequent to adoption (or of the issuance of a certificate of a Baptism which took place before adoption), the pastor should consult the local norms and legitimate practices, especially in the case of illegitimacy or of unknown parentage. Usually the fact of adoption should not be noted on any certificate of Baptism. The original birth certificate and other facts, if secured, should be placed in a secret register. Civil laws also must be kept in mind.

C. Subsequent Annotations

1. Confirmation

A notation of Confirmation received is to be made in the baptismal register.[236] It will suffice to record the date and place of celebration. There is thus indicated where other details can be found in case of necessity, e.g., in seeking proof of Catholic education. The pastor of the place of Confirmation is obliged to inform the pastor of the place of Baptism that this second sacrament has been conferred.

2. Matrimony

If Baptism was administered where the marriage is celebrated, the pastor has only to note in his own baptismal register the fact of the marriage. However, if the spouse (or spouses) was baptized elsewhere, the pastor of the place of marriage, either directly or through the episcopal curia, must inform the pastor of the place of Baptism of the fact of the marriage.[237] This latter pastor then makes an entry of the marriage in his own baptismal register. This procedure assures greater certainty in detecting matrimonial impediments. Should the marriage be later declared null by judicial process[238] or summary process, [239] or be dispensed either on the basis of *ratum et non-consummatum* or of solemn religious profession,[240] the registers are to be corrected in order to show the proper present

236. c. 470, 2.
237. Cf. **ibid.** and 1103, 2.
238. c. 1988.
239. c. 1990.
240. c. 1119.

status of the former contractants. The pastor is enabled to do this by reason of the notice sent to him by the Ordinary.

3. *Diaconate*

The local Ordinary or major religious superior is to send to the pastor of the place of Baptism notice to the effect that the diaconate has been received, and this is recorded in the baptismal register.[241] The initial reception of sacred orders must be noted, as it constitutes a diriment impediment to marriage. A later dispensation from Orders should also be noted.

4. *Solemn Profession*

The superior receiving the solemn religious profession must inform the pastor of the place of Baptism of this fact; this must be noted in the baptismal register.[242] This is a matrimonial impediment distinct from sacred orders and should be specifically recorded; likewise any subsequent dispensation from solemn vows.

D. *Baptismal Certificate*

1. The normal proof of Baptism is through the issuance of a baptismal certificate, which should be of recent date, i.e., issued within the last six months. It must contain all the necessary information as found in the register itself and be signed by the pastor of the place of issuance, or at least his name ought to be written on it and the one issuing the certificate countersign it, e.g., Reverend Henry Smith, pastor, per Reverend John Jones. The parish seal must be impressed on the certificate. This certificate enjoys the character of a legal public document, but it is full proof, however, of only the fact and date of Baptism and the identity of the minister and sponsors.[243] The pastor, moreover, in making entries into the baptismal record, is merely a public notary and not the judge of what is fitting or expedient. Thus, he is forbidden to make any

---

241. Cf. cc. 470, 2; 1011. Motu proprio **Ministeria quaedam,** 15 aug. 1972.
242. Cf. cc. 470, 2; 576, 2.
243. Cf. cc. 1813, 1, 4o; 1814.

changes without consulting the local Ordinary; likewise he cannot attest on a baptismal certificate information that differs from the register itself. A baptismal certificate from a non-Catholic sect does not constitute full proof of the reception of valid Baptism.

2. With children who are *legitimated* by the subsequent valid marriage of their parents, if this fact has been properly noted in the baptismal register,[244] a certificate of Baptism may be issued containing the names of both parents. Cases of children baptized before or after legal *adoption* are to be entered into the register in the manner required by canon 777 or referred to the local Ordinary. The same applies to the information to be certified on the issuance of the certificate. The local Ordinary must decide what changes, if any, may be permitted in cases which counsel concealment of the child's adoption. A true record of *illegitimacy* must be available when the baptized party wishes to enter into marriage, the religious life, or the priesthood. It does not seem that such information is necessary when a baptismal certificate is to be issued only for the purpose of testifying to the fact of Baptism, e.g., for entrance to a Catholic school, or for first Communion. The local Ordinary must decide in all such cases what information, if any, may be withheld or changed.

VIII. Juridic Rite of Affiliation by Baptism

The celebration of Baptism not only confers on the recipient personality in ecclesiastical law but at the same time usually determines the Catholic rite to which the same person becomes affiliated and must adhere.[245] This is true unless Baptism by chance was conferred by the minister of another rite either fraudulently or because of grave necessity when a priest of the candidate's rite was unavailable or when an Apostolic indult has permitted Baptism to be celebrated in a certain rite but without the juridic transfer of rite.[246]

244. Cf. above B 4 a.
245. cc. 87; 98, 1; Codex. Or., c. 6, 1.
246. c. 98, 1; Codex Or. c. 6, 2.

No baptized person may change from one rite to another, nor after a lawful change revert to the former rite, without permission of the Apostolic See (Congregation for the Oriental Churches).[247] A convert from an Orthodox Rite coming into the fullness of communion in the Catholic Church will thereupon belong to the corresponding Catholic Rite.[248] If, however, he wishes for sufficient reason to embrace a non-corresponding Catholic rite (e.g., the Latin Rite), permission should be sought from the Apostolic See.[249] It is common teaching that unbaptized adults upon entering the Church by Baptism may choose the rite to which they wish to adhere.[250]

The offspring should be baptized in the *rite of the parents*.[251] This is a serious obligation. Should the parents request a minister of another rite to baptize their offspring and he do so (legitimately or not), the offspring is affiliated to the rite in which he should have been baptized according to canon 756.[252] Thus, juridic affiliation to a rite by Baptism is not the rite in the ceremonies of which the individual was baptized, even in danger of death, but to the rite in the ceremonies of which he should have been baptized. The priest who performed the Baptism must send a record of it to the proper pastor.[253] The offspring of apostates are baptized according to the general rules. A foundling is baptized in the rite existing in the place where he was found.

If one of the parents belongs to the Latin Rite and the other to an Eastern Catholic Rite, the offspring is to be baptized in the *rite of the father*.[254] If only *one* of the parents is Catholic, the

---

247. c. 98, 3; Codex Or., c. 8, 1; Vatican II, Decree **Orientalium Ecclesiarum,** 4. For a wife changing her rite in marriage, cf. c. 98, 4; Codex. Or., c. 9.
248. **Orientalium Ecclesiarum,** 4: "Each and every Catholic, as well as the baptized members of every non-Catholic Church or community who enter into the fulness of Catholic communion, shall everywhere retain his proper rite, cherish it, and observe it to the best of his ability."
249. **Ibid.,** S.C.E.O., 24 mart. 1966.
250. Cf. Codex Or., c. 12.
251. c. 756, 1.
252. PCI 16 oct. 1919.
253. S.C.E.O. 1 mart. 1929.
254. c. 756, 2.

offspring is to be baptized in the rite of this parent.[255] It seems that, if the father is a member of a non-Catholic Eastern Church and the mother is a Latin or Eastern Catholic, and the father insists that the Baptism be celebrated in the Eastern Catholic rite corresponding to his, this may be done, with due permission, but without prejudice to the rite in which *de iure* the offspring belongs (i.e., the rite of the mother in this case. This is to be noted in the baptismal register and whenever a certificate is issued.) If the father, or in a mixed marriage, the Catholic mother, lawfully transfers to another rite, the minor children automatically also transfer to that rite.[256] Offspring which are illegitimate or posthumous or of non-Catholic paternity are baptized in the rite of the mother. If the father of the illegitimate child recognizes it in accordance with canon 777, 2, the offspring is baptized in the rite of the father.

IX. Liturgical Rite of Celebration

A. *Norms*

Baptism should be celebrated solemnly, i.e., with all the ceremonies and rites as presented in the approved liturgical books, except in the cases for private celebration provided for in the law.[257] This is a serious precept of the Church based upon due reverence for the sacrament. A minister sins seriously who, without proportionate cause, omits all the ceremonies or a notable one, changes them notably, or neglects a notable part of them. *No one*, not even a priest, may add, remove, or change anything in the liturgy *on his own authority*.[258]

255. **Ibid.,** 3.
256. Codex Or., cc. 10; 15.
257. cc. 755, 1; 737, 2.
258. **Sacrosanctum Concilium,** 22: "1. Regulation of the Sacred Liturgy depends solely on the authority of the Church, that is, on the Apostolic See, and, as laws may determine, on the bishops. 2. In virtue of power conceded by the law, the regulation of the liturgy within certain defined limits belongs

Adaptations in the liturgy of Baptism belongs to the competency of the Conference of Bishops or the local Ordinaries.[259] The minister of the celebration of Baptism may make those accomodations which are permitted to him in the liturgical rite itself.[260]

The norms and regulations of the Ordinary of the place regarding the liturgy of Baptism should be consulted. The catechumenate for adults is to be put into use *at the discretion of the local Ordinary*.[261] The celebration of Baptism may take place according to the Latin text or the vernacular text as approved by the Conference of Bishops.

B. *Structure*

1. *Children*

Baptism, whether for one child, or for several, or even for a large number, is celebrated by the ordinary minister and with the *full rite*, when there is no immediate danger of death.[262]

The *simpler rite* of Baptism is designed for the use of catechists when no priest or deacon is available.[263]

The *shorter rite* for use in *danger of death* and in the absence of the ordinary minister has a twofold structure: in imminent danger of death when only the water is poured and the customary formula pronounced, and if there is time some suggested ceremonies. The priest and deacon may likewise use this shorter form if necessary. If there is no time and he has the sacred chrism, the parish priest or other priest enjoying the same faculty is to

---

to various kinds of competent territorial bodies of Bishops legitimately established. 3. Therefore, absolutely no other person, not even a priest, may add, remove, or change anything in the liturgy on his own authority."

---

259. **Ordo Baptismi Parvulorum, Praenot. Gen.,** 31-33; **Praenot.,** 22-26; **Ordo initiationis Chrisianae adultorum,** 64-66.
260. **Ordo Baptismi Parvulorum, Praenot. Gen.,** 34-35; Praenot., 27-31; **Ordo initiationis Christianae adultorum,** 67.
261. **Sacrosanctum Concilium,** 64; **Ordo initiationis Christianae adultorum,** 44; 66; cf. also Vatican II, Decree **Ad gentes,** 14.
262. **Ordo Baptismi Parvulorum, Praenot.** 15; cf. chapters I, II, III.
263. **Ibid.,** 20; cf. ch. IV.

confer Confirmation after Baptism. In this case he omits the post-baptismal anointing with chrism.[264]

2. Adults

The rite of Christian initiation for adults comprises not only the celebration of the sacraments of Baptism, Confirmation, and the Eucharist but also all the rites of the catechumenate, which has been restored in the Church and which is under the direction of competent ecclesiastical authority.[265]

The *rite of the catechumenate arranged by steps* consists of the precatechumenate, catechumenate, period of purification and illumination, the admission to the sacraments, and the time of mystagogy.[266]

The *simpler rite of adult initiation* may be used in extraordinary circumstances (e.g., sickness, old age, change of residence, long trips, etc.,), when the candidate will not have been able to go through all the steps of initiation, or when the local Ordinary, having judged the candidate sincere in his Christian conversion and religiously mature, decides he may receive Baptism without delay and according to the arrangements of the simpler rite.[267]

The *shorter rite of adult initiation* is used for the Baptism of either catechumens or non-catechumens who are in danger of death and who can still hear and respond to questions, or who are at the moment of death, in which imminency the minister simply pours water and recites the customary formula.[268]

The *rite of initiation of youngsters who have reached the catechetical age* is designed for youngsters who have *not been baptized in infancy* and have reached the age of discretion and catechesis. Not being in the position to be treated as adults, they have been led to Christian initiation by their parents or guardians or they have spontaneously moved toward it but with the permission of their parents or guardians.[269]

264. **Ibid.,** 21-22.
265. **Ordo initiationis Christianae adultorum, Praenot., 2; 44.**
266. **Ibid.,** 6-40.
267. **Ibid.,** 240-244; 274-277.
268. **Ibid.,** 278-282.
269. **Ibid.,** 306-313.

Pastoral preparation for the admission to Confirmation and the Eucharist for those who have been baptized in infancy but received no catechesis is suggested in the Rite itself.[270]

Finally, there is the *rite of admission* of the *validly baptized* to full communion with the Catholic Church.[271]

3. Confirmation

The role of Confirmation in the baptismal liturgy is considered also in *The Celebration of Confirmation.*

a. Children

In danger of death, if there is time and he has the sacred chrism at hand, the pastor or other priest enjoying the same faculty is to confer Confirmation on the newly baptized. In this case he omits the postbaptismal anointing with chrism.[272]

b. Adults

Adults should receive Confirmation immediately after Baptism, unless graver reasons impede.[273]

4. Baptismal Name

In the Christian tradition the strong link between the person and the saint whose name he bears has always been favorably looked upon. It is a relationship of protection and, at the same time, an encouragement to reproduce the ideal of Christian life realized by the saint-protector.[274]

In the case of an adult the imposition of a Christian name has a particular significance. Baptism is in fact the beginning of a new life. On this account the change of name is most expressive of, so to speak, the change from the previous way of life to that

270. **Ordo initiationis Christianae adultorum,** 295-305.
271. **Ibid., Appendix,** 1-13.
272. **Ordo Baptismi Parvulorum, Praenot.,** 22; **Ordo Confirmationis** (S.C.C.D., 22 aug. 1971), **Praenot.** 11; 52.
273. **Ordo initiationis Christianae adultorum,** 34; 227-234; 266-270; 293; 361-365; **Ordo Confirmationis, Praenot.,** 11; 52.
274. **Notitiae,** 71 (March 1972), n. 2.

which is Christian.[275] However, for the adult candidate for Baptism the *Rite of Christian Initiation of Adults* allows[276] the imposition of a Christian name, or the giving of a "local" name which, however, has a Christian significance, or the retention by the candidate of the name which he already has, while explaining to him its Christian significance. The application of this to concrete cases is to be carried out by the Episcopal Conference.[277] The action regarding the name may take place at the beginning of the catechumenate or just before Baptism, according to the judgment of the Episcopal Conference.[278]

In the case of those receiving Baptism in infancy the dispositions of canon 761 continue to hold. Those who have already been baptized and have already assumed a Christian name may not subsequently change it,[279] at least no change of name can be entered into the baptismal register without the consent of ecclesiastical authority.

5. *Preliminary preparations*

Before the rite of the celebration of Baptism begins the minister should familiarize himself with the rite to be used, the actions and their order, the readings and prayers which may be selected, the materials for the ceremony that should be at hand.

All necessary information for the baptismal register should be obtained beforehand and written down, and any necessary instruction of the participants should be imparted. Inquiry should be made about the parochial domicile of the candidate, sex, possible emergency Baptism elsewhere and the date, by whom and according to what rite, the proposed name (the date of birth is not of itself necessary information).

Besides the names of the parents (maiden name of the mother), their domicile and rite, it is advisable to ascertain the date and place of their marriage, since sometimes a bad marriage is dis-

275. **Ibid.**
276. **Op. cit.,** 88; 203; 205.
277. **Ibid.**
278. **Ibid.,** Intr.; cf. **Ordo initiationis Christianae adultorum,** 88; 203.
279. **Ibid.,** 2.

covered and a convalidation may be initiated. The names and qualifications of the godparents are to be certified.

X. Admission of Converts to Full Communion

A. *General Notions*

A convert is one who, having been born and raised in beliefs
contrary to the teachings of the Catholic Church, is "led by the
Holy Spirit and by his own conscience"[280] to seek to embrace the
entire Catholic faith and to seek full membership in the society of
the Church. Local Ordinaries and pastors have an obligation toward
the non-Catholics in their territory to use every effort to bring about
their conversion.[281] In addition to efforts toward individuals, this
may be also pursued through information or instruction classes for
non-Catholics, study clubs, missions or retreats for non-Catholics,
adequate premarital instruction of the non-Catholic in a mixed marriage, etc. It should be noted that the apostolate of conversion with
regard to our non-Catholic or separated brethren in no way conflicts
with the dimension of pastoral concern and obligation which is
called ecumenism, and which in its Catholic teaching, should be
adequately understood and practiced.[282]

Prospective converts should be prudently questioned to ascertain
their motives in seeking information or instruction. Merely natural
motives in the beginning are not to be excluded as in the workings
of divine providence they often have their place in preparing a soul
with respect to good will. However, merely to please a spouse,
to acquire social or business or political advantage, etc., are insufficient or unworthy motives. True reasons for embracing the faith
should be urged. No one should be received into full communion
with the Church through Baptism or reconciliation who is not
intellectually prepared (according to age, condition, and capacity),

280. **Directorium,** 11 (Secr. ad unitatem Christianorum fovendam).
281. Cf. c. 1350, 1.
282. **Unitatis redintegratio,** 4; 5.

morally free and disposed by supernatural desires to embrace the entire faith and to observe its requirements (e.g., regarding marriage). Converts should receive a thorough instruction in the Commandments, the truths of the faith, the precepts of the Church, the sacraments, the obligations of their state in life, the practices of the Church, the virtues, the liturgy, etc. It is helpful to take the convert on a tour of the church and explain its contents. As soon as possible the person under instruction should be taught how to say daily prayers (including the Rosary) and to become accustomed to the practices of Catholic life, especially those of obligation, encouraged to hear sermons, assist at the liturgy, etc. A discreet inquiry about his marital status should be made early and any diriment impediment made known, even if it keeps him from joining the Church; also an inquiry about membership in any forbidden society. Diocesan norms and procedures concerning the instruction and the reception of converts should be consulted, e.g., the need to refer the Baptism of adults to the local Ordinary or the petition of the catechumen.

A follow-up of the newly received convert for a period after reception is very important, to be done either by the priest or a deacon or by laymen. Many converts lapse from the faith or its practices through lack of adequate help in deepening their faith and familiarity with the Church and its life. The leakage of converts from the Church reflects the need especially of a thorough preparation for entrance into the Church. The priest, moreover, must be most prudent in his contacts with women under instruction and with female neo-converts.

B. *Investigation of Baptism*

1. *Obligation*

Baptism is the sacramental bond of unity, indeed the foundation of communion among all Christians. Hence its dignity and the manner of administering it are matters of great importance to all Christ's disciples. Yet a just evaluation of the sacrament and the mutual recognition of each other's Baptisms by different communities is sometimes hindered because of a reasonable doubt about the Baptism conferred in some particular case.[283] The Church's practice in this matter is governed by two principles: that Baptism is necessary for salvation, and that it can be conferred only once.[284]

Thus it is absolutely necessary to determine if *de facto* Baptism has already taken place and, if so, whether it was a valid administration. No preconceived notions or presumptions that all non-Catholic Baptisms are invalid or doubtfully valid suffice.[285] Dogmatic errors do not of themselves make Baptism by non-Catholic ministers invalid.[286] Each case must be carefully considered to provide for the salvation of the soul and to guard against irreverence to the sacrament through a useless administration. Only moral impossibility excuses from such investigation. If nothing can be ascertained about the Baptism, at least conditional Baptism is necessary.

2. Fact of the Celebration of Baptism

a. Certification of the Celebration or Conferral

In the majority of cases proof of a previous *Catholic* Baptism can be obtained through the Baptismal certificate. In the absence of such public proof a private document can constitute a safe proof, e.g., a personal letter of the pastor certifying his conferral of Baptism on the subject. However, the authorship of such a document and the credibility of its content must be determined. The same is true of a document intended as a public one but lacking authenticity by reason of the omission of some legal formality, e.g., lacking the impression of the parochial seal.

Regarding *non-Catholics,* if the convert was born and raised in a sect not observing the rite of Baptism and if he never joined one that baptizes, there is sufficient evidence that he was never baptized. If he belonged to a sect that baptizes, a certificate from this sect is not acceptable as full proof of the reception of Baptism (or of its validity), having the probative value of a private document. Yet, if judged to be genuine and credible and if supported

283. **Directorium, loc. cit.**
284. **Ibid., 9.**
285. S. Off. 20 nov. 1878; S.C.P.F. 26 iun. 1845; S.C. Conc. 27 mart. 1683; S. Off. 6 apr 1859; 21 feb. 1883.
286. S. Off. 28 dec. 1949.

by other evidence confirmatory of this certificate, it would be acceptable.[287]

b. *Subsidiary Methods of Certification*

At times a public document to prove the reception of Baptism may not be obtainable. In such cases, testimonial evidence may be used to establish the fact. A *qualified witness* is a public official who is designated by law to testify to those acts which he executed or witnessed in the performance of the duties of his office. In the case of *Catholic* Baptism the pastor is such a witness if he conferred the sacrament himself or was present at the administration or celebration. If such a pastor testifies in favor of a Baptism, his testimony constitutes full legal proof. If the pastor has authorized another to administer the sacrament, the latter's testimony would be equivalent to that of a pastor. In an analogous manner, the non-Catholic minister of Baptism is a more certain witness of the fact of Baptism but not, thereby, of its validity, nor does his certification constitute full proof, as noted above.

Besides the one who baptized, *other witnesses* who attended the ceremony could testify to confirm the reception of Baptism. When two or more such witnesses testify to the celebration or administration, their declaration could constitute full legal proof.[288] Unless there is a question of a qualified witness, the deposition of *one witness* ordinarily does not afford full proof. Canonical jurisprudence, however, admits certain exceptions. Thus, when there is question of determining the Baptism of a party, the testimony of one witness who is above all suspicion is sufficient to prove that the sacrament was conferred, provided that his testimony does not redound to another's prejudice.[289] A person above suspicion is one who is absolutely trustworthy and whose testimony is not to be excluded by reason of unfitness, suspicion, or incapacity.[290] The

287. Cf. Rota, **Decisiones,** III (1911), 26-263.
288. Cf. c. 1791, 2.
289. c. 779.
290. Cf. c. 1757.

testimony of such a witness will not be prejudicial to another if the established fact of Baptism does not run counter to the best interests of another, e.g., the nullity of a marriage dependent upon Baptism.

The sworn *oath* of the *party baptized* is final source of proof. That this oath be acceptable, the claim to Baptism must not be prejudicial to the right of another and the Baptism must have been received as an adult.[291] In arriving at a judgment of the fact (or validity) of Baptism in the procedure of the reception of a convert, the priest will evaluate the testimony and even the oath given. If there still remains any prudent doubt the sacrament will be conferred conditionally.

3. *Validity of Baptism*

This will depend upon the presence of the required material, formula, and intention of the minister and the recipient. The investigation will include an examination of the ritual of the sect in which the convert was baptized. If the ritual prescribes a valid material and formula, or one which is of doubtful validity, (e.g., by way of sprinkling, especially of several people at once), or which is clearly invalid, the initial presumption will likewise correspond. If the ritual is lacking or unobtainable, the investigation will cover the required material, formula, and intention. Moreover, the use of the ritual should be investigated to determine if the minister actually conformed to the ritual of his sect.[292]

There can be no doubt cast upon the validity of Baptism as conferred among *separated Eastern Christians*. It is enough, therefore, to establish the fact that Baptism was administered.[293]

In respect of *other Christians* a doubt can sometimes arise:

a) Concerning the required material and the formula. Baptism by immersion, pouring, or sprinkling, together with the

291. Cf. c. 779.
292. S. Off. 28 dec. 1949. The presumption of the Holy Office of valid intention for Baptism among Baptists, Disciples of Christ, Presbyterians, Congregationalists, Methodists, pertains only to judgment in **matrimonial** cases.
293. **Directorium,** 12.

Trinitarian formula, is of itself valid. Therefore, if the rituals and liturgical books or established customs of a church or community prescribe one of these ways of baptizing, doubt can only arise if it happens that the minister does not observe the regulations of his own community or church. What is necessary and sufficient, therefore, is evidence that the minister of Baptism was faithful to the norms of his own community or church. For this purpose generally one should obtain a written baptismal certificate with the name of the minister. In many cases the other community may be asked to cooperate in establishing whether or not, in general or in a particular case, a minister is to be considered as having baptized according to the approved ritual.

b) Concerning faith and intention. Because some consider that insufficiency of faith or intention in the minister can create a doubt about Baptism, these points should be noted: 1) the minister's insufficient faith never of itself makes Baptism invalid; 2) Sufficient intention in a baptizing minister is to be presumed unless there is serious ground for doubting that he intends to do what Christians do.[294]

C. Procedure for Reception of Converts

1. Unbaptized

When the serious investigation establishes the fact that the prospective convert has not received Baptism at all or that it was certainly invalid, he is admitted into the Church through the celebration of Baptism according to the appropriate liturgical rite.

2. Doubtfully baptized

Indiscriminate conditional Baptism of all who desire full communion with the Catholic Church cannot be approved. The sacrament of Baptism cannot be repeated and, therefore, to baptize again conditionally is not allowed, unless there is prudent doubt of the fact, or the validity of a Baptism already administered. If after serious investigation as to whether the Baptism was properly admin-

294. **Ibid.,** 13.

istered a reasonable doubt persists, and it is necessary to baptize conditionally, the minister should maintain proper regard for the doctrine that Baptism is unique by: a) suitably explaining both why he is in this case baptizing conditionally and what is the significance of the rite of conditional Baptism; b) carrying out the rite according to the private form.[295]

In the case of the truly doubtfully baptized the order of admission is: a) profession of faith according to the regulations of the local Ordinary; b) conditional Baptism celebrated in private form; c) confession of sins with conditional absolution.

3. *Validly Baptized*

The validly baptized entering full Catholic communion are obliged only to: a) profession of faith according to the regulations of the local Ordinary; b) confession of sins with absolution. The absolution from excommunication and the abjuration of error is obligatory only for baptized *Catholics* seeking reconciliation with the Church. "The Decree on Ecumenism makes clear that the brethren born and baptized outside the visible communion of the Catholic Church should be carefully distinguished from those who, though baptized in the Catholic Church, have knowingly and publicly abjured her faith. According to the decree one cannot charge with the sin of separation those who at present are born into these communities and in them are brought up in the faith of Christ. Hence, in the absence of such blame, if they freely wish to embrace the Catholic faith, they have no need to be absolved from excommunication, but after making profession of their faith according to the regulations set down by the Ordinary of the place they should be admitted into the full communion of the Catholic Church. What canon 2314 prescribed is only applicable to those who, after culpably giving up the Catholic faith or communion, repent and ask to be reconciled with Mother Church. What has just been said of absolution from censures obviously applies for the same reason to the abjuring of heresy."[296]

295. **Ibid.**, 14-15.
296. **Ibid.**, 19-20.

THE CELEBRATION OF CONFIRMATION

I. Confirmation, a Second Degree of Christian Initiation

Confirmation, the Christian's personal Pentecost, is the complement of Baptism, the strengthening and perfecting of the Christian life inaugurated in Baptism and to be consummated in the Eucharist. Those who have been baptized continue the path of Christian initiation through the sacrament of Confirmation in which they receive the Holy Spirit poured out, the same Spirit who was sent upon the Apostles by the Lord on the day of Pentecost. This gift of the Holy Spirit conforms believers more perfectly to Christ and strengthens them so that they may bear witness to Christ for the building up of his body in faith and love. They are so marked with the character or seal of the Lord that the sacrament of Confirmation cannot be repeated.[1]

Through the sacrament of Confirmation those who have been born anew in Baptism receive the inexpressible Gift, the Holy Spirit himself, by which "they are endowed ... with special strength," and, having been sealed with the character of this same sacrament, are "bound more intimately to the Church" and "are more strictly obliged to spread and defend the faith both by word and by deed as true witnesses of Christ."[2]

As we require the grace of Baptism to form the mind unto faith, so it is of the utmost advantage that the souls of the faithful be strengthened by a different grace, to the end that they be deterred by no danger, or fear of pains, tortures, or death, from the confession of the true faith.[3] Inasmuch as they are reborn as sons of God, the faithful must confess before men the faith which they have received from God through the Church. Then, bound more intimately to the Church by the sacrament of Confirmation, they are endowed by the Holy Spirit with special strength. Hence they

1. **Ordo Confirmationis, Praenotanda,** 1-2 (S.C. pro Cultu Divino, 22 aug. 1971).
2. Const. Apost. **Divinae consortium naturae,** 15 aug. 1971.
3. **Catechism of the Council of Trent** (ed. McHugh & Callan), p. 201.

are more strictly obliged to spread and defend the faith both by word and deed as true witnesses of Christ.[4] And so, the sacrament by which spiritual strength is conferred on the one born again makes him in some sense a front-line fighter for the faith of Christ.[5] For wherever they live, all Christians are bound to show forth, by the example of their lives and by the witness of their speech, that new man which they put on at Baptism and that power of the Holy Spirit by whom they were strengthened at Confirmation. Thus other men, observing their good works, can glorify the Father and can better appreciate the real meaning of human life and the bond which ties the whole community of mankind together.[6]

It is of faith that Confirmation is a true and distinct sacrament of the New Law,[7] that it confers on the soul an indelible character and thus it may not be repeated.[8] Confirmation is not necessary for salvation by any necessity of means or precept,[9] but it is morally necessary for the Christian. Being a divinely instituted means of perfecting the way of salvation, it may not be neglected. A failure to seek Confirmation when it is opportune is of itself a slight sin, but it can become serious by reason of scandal, contempt, or special spiritual need. Those with the care of souls should see to it that all the baptized come to the fullness of Christian initiation and therefore are carefully prepared for Confirmation.[10]

II. Requirements for the celebration of Confirmation

A. Requisite material

The only valid material for the celebration of Confirmation is sacred chrism, that is, pure olive oil mixed with balsam and blessed

4. Const. Dogm. **Lumen gentium,** 11.
5. St. Thomas, **IV Cont. Gent.,** c. 60; cf. also **Summa Theol.,** III, q. 72, a. 1.
6. Decr. **Ad gentes,** 11.
7. **Enchiridion Symbolorum,** Denz.-Schön. 1628; cf. also 860, 1317, 3444.
8. **Ibid.,** 1609; cf. also 1313.
9. CIC, c. 787.
10. **Ordo Confirm., Praenot.,** 3; c. 787.

by the bishop.[11] When the amount of chrism is too far diminished, other olive oil should be added, even repeatedly, but in a lesser quantity.[12] The chrism (S.C.) is consecrated by the bishop in the Mass which is ordinarily celebrated on Holy Thursday for this purpose.[13] It is never allowed to administer Confirmation without chrism or to receive the chrism from bishops not in communion with the Apostolic See.[14]

B. *Proper use of the material*

Through the anointing with chrism on the forehead, which is done by the imposition of the hand (together with the formula), the sacrament is conferred.[15] The making of the sign of the cross while anointing with the chrism is necessary for validity.[16] No instrument may be employed in the anointing, but the right hand itself (the four fingers) is directly laid on the forehead and the anointing is made with the right thumb.[17] To use any finger (even of the left hand) other than the right thumb in anointing, without justifying cause, would be a slight sin but not invalidating. Validity requires only the imposition of the hand which accompanies the unction. Even though the imposition of hands upon the candidates with the

11. Denz.-Schön., 1317; **Ordo Confirm., Praenot.,** 9; S.C.C.D., 3 dec. 1970, **Ordo benedicendi oleum catechumenorum et infirmorum ac conficienda chrisma, Praenot.,** 3: "Apt material of a sacrament is olive oil or, according to opportunity, another plant oil"; 4· "Chrism is made up of oil and spices or fragrant material"; 2: "By sacred chrism it is demonstrated that Christians, having been inserted in the Paschal mystery of Christ by Baptism, have died, been buried, and risen with him, are sharers in his royal and prophetical priesthood, and receive through Confirmation the spiritual unction of the Holy Spirit who is given to them."
12. Cf. cc. 734; 781.
13. **Ordo Confirm., Praenot.,** 10; **Ordo benedic.,** 9-10.
14. Cf. S.C. Sac. "Spiritus Sancti munera," 14 sept. 1946; Secr. ad unitatem Christianorum fovendam, **Directorium,** 14 maii 1967, 38-55, here makes no mention of Confirmation in the sharing in liturgical worship.
15. **Ordo Confirm, Praenot.,** 9.
16. S.C. Rit., 7 mai 1853.
17. c. 781; S.Off. 14 ian. 1885.

prayer *All-powerful God* does not pertain to the valid conferral of the sacrament, it is to be strongly emphasized for the integrity of the rite and the fuller understanding of the sacrament.[18]

C. *Required words or Formula*

The formula in the conferral of Confirmation is: *N., Be sealed with the Holy Spirit, the Gift of the Father.*[19] Thus the Latin Church adopts the very ancient formula belonging to the Byzantine Rite, by which the Gift of the Holy Spirit himself is expressed and the outpouring of the Spirit which took place on the day of Pentecost is recalled.[20]

D. *Time and place of the celebration of Confirmation*

The sacrament of Confirmation may be conferred or celebrated at any time of the year, although Pentecost is most fitting.[21] Ordinarily Confirmation takes place within the Mass in order to express more clearly the fundamental connection of this sacrament with the entirety of Christian initiation.[22]

Although the appropriate place for the celebration of the rite of Confirmation is a church, especially because of its normal celebration within the Mass, it may be celebrated in any other worthy place, for a just and reasonable cause in the judgment of the minister,[23] e.g., in danger of death. In his diocese the Bishop has the right to confirm even in exempt places including the churches of regulars.[24]

1. *For children*

In the Latin Church the administration or celebration of Con-

---

18. **Ordo Confirm., Praenot.,** 9; cf. S.Off. 17 apr. 1872; 22 mart. 1892.
19. **Ordo Confirm., ibid.**
20. **Divinae consortium naturae.**
21. c. 790. The **Missa Ritualis in conferenda Confirmatione** may be used on any day except the Sundays of Advent, Lent, and Easter, solemnities, Ash Wednesday, and Holy Week (**Missale Romanum,** p. 736).
22. **Ordo Confirm., Praenot.,** 13.
23. c. 791.
24. c. 792; S.Off. 16 iun. 1884.

firmation is generally postponed until about the seventh year. For pastoral reasons, however, especially to strengthen in the life of the faithful complete obedience to Christ the Lord in loyal testimony to him, episcopal conferences may choose an age which appears more appropriate, so that the sacrament is conferred after appropriate formation at a more mature age.[25]

There should always be the necessary concern that children be confirmed at the proper time, even before the use of reason, when there is danger of death or other serious difficulty. They should not be deprived of the benefit of this sacrament.[26] In the case of a child who has not yet reached the age of reason, Confirmation is conferred in accordance with the same principles and norms as Baptism.[27]

If the candidates for Confirmation are children who have not received the Eucharist and are not admitted to their First Communion at this liturgical celebration or in other special circumstances, Confirmation is celebrated outside of Mass. When this occurs, there should first be a celebration of the word of God.[28]

2. *For adults and youths of catechetical age*

Adults should receive Confirmation immediately after Baptism, unless graver reasons impede. By this connection there are signified the unity of the Paschal mystery, the intimate relationship between the mission of the Son and the pouring forth of the Holy Spirit, and the union of the sacraments by which each divine person with the Father comes to the baptized.[29]

The rite of Confirmation reaches its culmination in the communion of the Body and Blood of Christ. Therefore, the newly-confirmed should share in the Eucharist which completes their Christian initiation.[30]

25. **Ordo Confirm., Praenot.,** 11.
26. **Ibid.;** also 52. Cf. **Ordo Baptismi Parvulorum,** Praenot., 22.
27. **Ordo Confirm., Praenot.,** 52.
28. **Ibid.,** 13.
29. **Ordo initiationis christianae adultorum,** 34; 227-234; 266-270; 293; 361-365; **Ordo Confirm.,** 11; 53.
30. **Ordo Confirm., Praenot.,** 13. If First Communion was received, then the frequent reception of Communion may not be prevented (S.C. Sac. 30 iun. 1932; cf. also 20 maii 1934).

Confirmation must be received before entering the novitiate of a religious institute,[31] or the clerical state,[32] and, if possible, before marriage.[33]

A sick person in danger of death should be strengthened by Confirmation before he receives the Eucharist as Viaticum, after the requisite and possible catechesis. In danger of death, however, the sacraments of Confirmation and Anointing of the Sick are not *ordinarily* to be celebrated in the same rite.[34] When circumstances permit, the Rite of Confirmation outside Mass is followed.[35]

III. Minister of the Celebration of Confirmation

A. *Original minister*

The original or ordinary minister of Confirmation is the Bishop.[36] Normally the sacrament is celebrated by the Bishop so that there will be a more evident relationship to the first pouring forth of the Holy Spirit on the day of Pentecost. After they were filled with the Holy Spirit, the Apostles themselves gave the Spirit to the faithful through the laying on of their hands. In this way the reception of the Spirit through the ministry of the Bishop shows the close bond which joins the confirmed to the Church as well as the mandate of Christ to be witnesses among men.[37]

---

31. c. 544, 1.
32. cc. 974, 1, 1o; 933, 1o.
33. c. 1021, 2.
34. **Ordo Confirm.,** 52. However, when it is necessary to confer all the sacraments in danger of death in one continual rite, Confirmation is conferred immediately before the blessing of the oil of the Infirm (S.C.D., 7 dec. 1972, **Ordo unctionis infirmorum eorumque pastoralis curae,** 117, 124, 136-137).
35. **Ibid.,** 53.
36. It is of faith that only a consecrated Bishop is the ordinary minister of Confirmation (Denz.-Schön. 1630; cf. c. 782, 1) by the very power of ordination itself and not by any special papal commission.
37. **Ordo Confirm Praenot.,** 7.

Within his own territory the Bishop confirms lawfully even one who is not his own subject, unless the latter's own Ordinary has expressly forbidden it. Outside his own territory he needs at least the presumed permission of the local Ordinary, except to confirm his own subjects privately and without the use of mitre and crozier.[38] To act in violation of these provisions would be valid but seriously unlawful.

A Bishop is bound to confirm his subjects who properly and reasonably request this sacrament, especially during his pastoral visitation,[39] or to see to it that the sacrament is provided.[40] Of its nature this is a serious obligation in justice; it admits, however, of lightness of matter. The ample provisions for extraordinary ministers in the Apostolic Constitution *Divinae consortium naturae* greatly assist the Bishop in the fulfillment of his obligation to provide the sacrament for the faithful. To neglect or to refuse habitually to administer Confirmation would certainly be a serious sin.

B. *Other ministers*

In addition to the Bishop, the *law* gives the faculty to confirm to the following:[41]

1) apostolic administrators who are not bishops, prelates or abbots *nullius*, vicars and prefects apostolic, vicars capitular, within the limits of their territory and while they are in office;

2) priests who, in virtue of an office they lawfully hold, baptize an *adult* or a *child old enough for catechesis*, or who admit a validly baptized *adult* into full communion with the Church.

N.B. The priest who baptizes an *adult* or a *youngster of catechetical age* may, in the absence of the Bishop, also confer Confirmation, unless this sacrament should be conferred at another time. When the number to be confirmed is large, the minister of Confirmation may associate with himself other priests to administer the sacrament. It is necessary that these priests:

38. c. 783.
39. c. 875, 1.
40. **Ibid.,** 3; cf. also c. 343, 1.
41. **Ordo Confirm, Praenot.** 7.

a) either enjoy a function of office in the diocese, namely, vicar general, episcopal vicar or delegate, district or regional vicar, or one which by the mandate of the Ordinary is considered ex officio equal to these;

b) or are pastors of the places in which Confirmation is celebrated, or pastors of the places to which those to be confirmed pertain, or are priests who have performed some special work in the catechetical preparation of those to be confirmed.[42]

3) *in danger of death,* provided a Bishop is not easily available or is lawfully impeded: pastors and parochial vicars; in their absence, their parochial associates; priests who are in charge of special parishes lawfully established; administrators; substitutes; and assistants. In the absence of all the preceding, any priest who is not subject to censure or canonical penalty.

N.B. In danger of death of *children,* if there is time and he has the sacred chrism at hand, the parish priest or other priest enjoying the same faculty is to confer Confirmation on the newly baptized. In this case he omits the postbaptismal anointing with chrism.[43]

By special *Apostolic indult* a priest may be granted the habitual faculty to confirm, e.g., a vicar general or chancellor, in order to assist with the large number of confirmations in a diocese or on account of distances, etc.[44]

All the above-mentioned ministers of Confirmation may, in case of true necessity and special reason, for example, the large number of persons to be confirmed, associate other priests with themselves in the celebration of this sacrament.[45]

When Confirmation is conferred or celebrated by a minister who is not a Bishop, whether by concession of the general law or by special indult of the Apostolic See, he should mention in the homily that the Bishop is the original minister of the sacrament. He should explain why a priest receives the faculty to confirm from the law or by an indult of the Apostolic See.

42. **Ordo initiationis christianae adultorum, Praenot.,** 46.
43. **Ordo Bap. Parvul., Praenot.,** 22; cf. **Ordo Confirm., Intro.,** 11; 52.
44. **Ordo Confirm., Praenot.,** 8; cf. c. 782, 2.
45. **Ibid.,** 8.

The priest who enjoys by law or Apostolic privilege the faculty to confirm is under the obligation to administer this sacrament to those for whom the faculty has been granted, whenever they properly and reasonably request it.[46] His obligation, however, is not more binding than that of the Bishop himself.

IV. Candidates for Confirmation

One must be baptized in order validly to receive the sacrament of Confirmation. In addition, if the baptized person has the use of reason, it is required (for lawfulness and fruitfulness) that he be in the state of grace, properly instructed, and able to renew his baptismal promises.[47]

An implicit habitual intention suffices for adults. The sacrament revives when an obstacle of serious sin impeding its effect is removed. Those not in full communion with the Church may not be confirmed until they first become reconciled to the Church.

It is the responsibility of the episcopal conferences to determine more precisely the pastoral means for the preparation of children for Confirmation.[48]

Adults should receive Confirmation immediately after Baptism, unless graver reasons impede.[49] In their regard, the same principles should be followed, with suitable adaptations, which are in effect in individual dioceses for the admission of catechumens to Baptism and the Eucharist. In particular, suitable catechesis should precede Confirmation. The relationship of the candidates with the Christian community and with individual members of the faithful should be sufficiently effective to assist them in their formation. This should be directed toward their living the witness of a Christian life and

---

46. c. 785, 2.
47. **Ordo Confirm., Praenot., 12; c. 786.**
48. **Ibid.**
49. **Ordo initiationis christianae adultorum, Praenot., 34.**

exercising the Christian apostolate, while developing a genuine desire to participate in the Eucharist.[50]

It sometimes happens that the preparation of a baptized adult for Confirmation is part of his preparation for marriage. In such cases, if it is foreseen that the conditions for a fruitful reception of Confirmation will not be satisfied, the local Ordinary will judge whether or not it is better to defer Confirmation until after the marriage.[51]

If one who has the use of reason is confirmed in danger of death, he should be prepared spiritually, so far as possible, depending upon the circumstances of the individual case.[52]

Where it is customary for the candidate of Confirmation to receive a new name,[53] even when Confirmation immediately follows Baptism, this request for a new name should be granted. The new name is recorded in the proper place in the Confirmation register.

V. Sponsors at the celebration of Confirmation

Ordinarily there should be a sponsor for each of those to be confirmed. The sponsor brings the candidate to receive the sacrament, presents him to the minister for anointing, and will later help him to fulfill his baptismal promises faithfully under the influence of the Holy Spirit.[54] It is more generally considered that the obligation to have a sponsor or godparent is serious,[55] but less so than at Baptism.

In view of contemporary pastoral circumstances, it is desirable that the godparent at Baptism, if present, also be the sponsor at

---

50. **Ordo Confirm., loc. cit.; Ordo initiationis christianae adultorum,** 19.
51. **Ordo Confirm., loc. cit.**
52. **Ibid.**
53. S.C. Rit. 20 sept. 1749, ad 7.
54. **Ordo Confirm., Praenot., 5; c. 793.**
55. Cf. S. Off. 5 sept. 1877.

Confirmation. This expresses more clearly the relationship between Baptism and Confirmation and also makes the duty and function of the sponsor or godparent more effective.[56] Nonetheless, the choice of a special sponsor for Confirmation is not excluded. Even the parents themselves may present their children for Confirmation. It is the responsibility of the local Ordinary to determine diocesan practice in the light of local circumstances.[57]

Pastors should see to it that the sponsor or godparent, chosen by the candidate or his family, is spiritually qualified for the office and a) sufficiently mature for this role, b) belongs to the Catholic Church and himself already initiated into the three sacraments of Baptism, Confirmation, and the Eucharist, c) and not prohibited by law from exercising the role of sponsor.[58]

The sponsor must place his right hand on the shoulder of the one to be confirmed at the time of the anointing by the Bishop or minister of Confirmation.[59]

Valid Confirmation gives rise to a spiritual relationship between sponsor and the one confirmed, binding the sponsor or godparent to regard the one confirmed as permanently committed to his care and to safeguard his Christian education. This spiritual relationship does not establish an impediment to marriage.[60]

VI. Confirmation register and certificate

The pastor should record the names of the minister, those confirmed, parents and sponsors, the date and place of Confirmation in a special book or Confirmation register, in addition to the notation in the baptismal register which is made according to law.[61]

---

56. **Ordo Confirm., Praenot.,** 5.
57. **Ibid.**
58. **Ibid.,** 6; cf. c. 795, 1o, 2o, 5o; 796, 3o.
59. **Ordo Confirm., Praenot.,** 26; 43.
60. cc. 797; 1079.
61. **Ordo Confirm. Praenot.,** 14.

If the proper pastor of the newly confirmed is not present, the minister should inform him of the Confirmation either personally or through a representative.[62] This is usually done by way of the Confirmation certificate.

VII. Liturgical rite of Confirmation

A. *Norms*

In the liturgy of Confirmation attention should be paid to the festive and solemn character of the liturgical service, especially its significance for the local church. It is appropriate for all the candidates to be assembled for a common celebration. The whole people of God, represented by the families and friends of the candidates and by members of the local community, should be invited to take part in the celebration and to express its faith in the gifts of the Holy Spirit.[63]

It is fitting that the minister of Confirmation celebrate the Mass, or, better, concelebrate the Mass, especially with the priests who may lawfully join him in the administration of the sacrament. If the Mass is celebrated by someone else, it is proper that the Bishop preside over the liturgy of the word and that he give the blessing at the end of Mass.[64]

Emphasis should be given to the celebration of the word of God which begins the rite of Confirmation. It is from the hearing of the word of God that the diverse activity of the Holy Spirit flows upon the Church and upon each one of the baptized and the confirmed, and it is by this word that God's will is manifest in the life of Christians.[65]

The recitation of the Lord's Prayer by the newly confirmed with the rest of the people is also of very great importance, whether

62. Ibid., 15.
63. Ibid., 4.
64. Ibid., 13.
65. Ibid., 13.

during Mass before Communion or outside Mass before the blessing, because it is the Spirit who prays in us, and the Christian in the Spirit says: Abba, Father.[66]

Episcopal conferences have the right to make certain adaptations in the liturgy of Confirmation.[67] The minister of Confirmation may introduce some comments into the rite in individual cases and in view of the nature of the candidates for Confirmation. He may also make appropriate accomodations in the existing texts, for example, by expressing these in a kind of dialogue, especially with children.[68] Beyond this no addition, subtraction, or change may be made in the liturgy of Confirmation on one's own authority.[69]

B. *Structure*

The liturgy of Confirmation provides a rite of celebration within Mass[70] and outside Mass.[71] In danger of death the entire rite should be observed, if circumstances permit; otherwise a shortened rite is used.[72] In case of extreme necessity, it suffices that only the anointing be done together with the sacramental formula.[73]

66. **Ibid.,**
67. **Ibid.,** 16; 17.
68. **Ibid.,** 18.
69. Cf. Const. **Sacrosanctum Concilium,** 22.
70. **Ordo Confirm., Praenot.,** 20-33.
71. **Ibid.,** 34-49.
72. **Ibid.,** 52-55.
73. **Ibid.,** 56.

THE CELEBRATION OF THE EUCHARIST

I. The Eucharist, Fulfillment and Unity in Christ

A. Initiation into Christ and his Church are brought to completion and fulfillment in the Eucharist.[1] Thus all the sacraments are directed to the Eucharist: Baptism and Confirmation as the initiation and strengthening in the Christian life, Penance and the Anointing of the Sick as purifying from sin and its residue whereby the baptized are made worthy participants in the Eucharist, Holy Orders by which an ordained priesthood is provided in every generation to continue the Eucharist, Matrimony by which members for the common priesthood of the true worshippers are handed down.

The Eucharist is both sacrament and sacrifice and thus exercises a twofold inseparable role. At the Last Supper on the night when he was betrayed, our Savior instituted the Eucharistic Sacrifice of His Body and Blood. He did this in order to perpetuate the sacrifice of the Cross throughout the centuries until he should come again, and so to entrust to his beloved spouse, the Church, a memorial of his death and resurrection: a sacrament of love, a sign of unity, a bond of charity, a paschal banquet in which Christ is consumed, the mind is filled with grace, and a pledge of future glory is given to us.[2]

The Eucharist is a very great mystery,[3] a mystery which Christ the High Priest instituted and which he commanded to be continually renewed in the Church by his ministers, and which is culmination and center, as it were, of the Christian religion.[4] It is in

1. "The other sacraments, as well as every ministry of the Church and every work of the apostolate, are linked with the Holy Eucharist and are directed toward it. For the most blessed Eucharist contains the Church's entire spiritual wealth, that is, Christ himself, our Passover and living bread" (Vatican II, Decree **Presbyterorum Ordinis,** 5).
2. Vatican II, Const. **Sacrosanctum Concilium,** 47.
3. Paul VI, enc. **Mysterium fidei** (3 sept. 1965), 15.
4. Pius XII, enc. **Mediator Dei** (20 nov. 1947), 66. Vatican II, Const. **Lumen gentium,** 11: "the Eucharistic sacrifice is the fount and

the Eucharist that the close union of the Mystical Body of Jesus Christ with its Head reaches during this mortal life, as it were, its completion.[5] Thus in the sacrament of the Eucharistic bread the unity of all believers who form one body in Christ is both expressed and brought about.[6] Celebrating the Eucharistic Sacrifice we are, therefore, most closely united to the worshipping Church in heaven.[7] Truly partaking of the body of the Lord in the breaking of the Eucharistic bread, we are taken up into communion with him and with one another.[8]

The Eucharist is the source of perfecting the Church.[9] The life of the Church grows through persistent participation in the Eucharistic mystery.[10] No Christian community can be built up unless it has its basis and center in the celebration of the most holy Eucharist.[11] The renewal in the Eucharist of the covenant between the Lord and man draws the faithful into the compelling love of Christ and sets them afire. From the liturgy, therefore, and especially from the Eucharist, as from a fountain, grace is channeled to us; and the sanctification of man in Christ and the glorification of God, to which all other activities of the Church are directed as toward their goal, are most powerfully achieved.[12] Thus the Lord left behind a pledge of hope and strength for life's journey in that sacrament of faith where natural elements refined by man are changed into his glorified Body and Blood, providing a meal of

apex of the whole Christian life." Cf. ibid., Decree **Unitatis redintegratio,** 15.

---

5. **Ibid.,** 81.
6. Cf. Vatican II, Decree **Unitatis redintegratio,** 2.
7. **Ibid.,** 50.
8. **Ibid.,** 7.
9. Vatican II, Decree **Ad gentes,** 39. "The mystery of the Eucharist is the true center of the sacred liturgy, and indeed of the whole Christian life. Consequently the Church, guided by the Holy Spirit, continually seeks to understand and to live the Eucharist more fully" (S.C. Rit., 25 maii 1967, Instr. **Eucharisticum mysterium**).
10. Vatican II, Const. **Dei Verbum,** 26.
11. **Presbyterorum Ordinis,** 6.
12. **Sacrosanctum Concilium,** 10.

brotherly solidarity and a foretaste of the heavenly banquet.[13]

Through the ministry of priests the spiritual sacrifice of the faithful is made perfect in union with the sacrifice of Christ, the sole Mediator. Through the hands of the priest and in the name of the whole Church the Lord's sacrifice is offered in the Eucharist in an unbloody and sacramental manner until he himself returns.[14] In discharging their duty to sanctify their people, pastors of souls should arrange for the celebration of the Eucharistic Sacrifice to be the center and culmination of the whole life of the Christian community.[15]

B. The word "eucharist" comes from the Greek εὐχαριστειυ signifying "to give thanks,"[16] which thanks are due because of the great benefit, the good grace (derived also from the same Greek root), which it confers, containing as it does the Author of grace. In its daily consecration thanksgiving is offered to God for benefits received and for the very institution of the sacrament itself. Many other terms have also been used in Scripture and in Tradition to refer to the divine sacrament and sacrifice.[17]

"This sacrament has a threefold significance: one with regard to the past inasmuch as it is commemorative of Our Lord's Passion, which was a true sacrifice..., and in this respect it is called a *sacrifice*. With regard to the present it has another meaning, that of ecclesiastical unity in which men are aggregated through this sacrament; and in this respect it is called *communion* or σύναξις. With regard to the future it has a third meaning, inasmuch as this sacrament foreshadows the divine fruition, which shall come to pass in heaven; and according to this it is called *viaticum* because it

---

13. Vatican II, Const. **Gaudium et spes,** 38. "Through the mystery of the Eucharist the sacrifice of the Cross, which was once offered on Calvary, is remarkably re-enacted and constantly recalled, and its saving power exerted for the forgiveness of those sins we daily commit" (**Mysterium fidei,** 27).
14. **Presbyterorum Ordinis,** 2.
15. Vatican II, Decree **Christus Dominus,** 30.
16. Cf. I Cor. 11:24.
17. Cf. e.g., Jn. 6:32, 35, 51; Acts 2:42; I Cor. 10:16; 11:20, 23-24; agape, consecration, mystery of faith, sacred mystery, etc.

supplies the way of reaching there.... It is termed a *host* inasmuch as it contains Christ who is 'a host ... of sweetness'."[18]

The Eucharist is thus a sacrament of the New Law as instituted by Christ in which under the consecrated species of bread and wine the Body and Blood of Christ are truly, really, and substantially contained, for the purpose of producing grace after the manner of a spiritual nourishment. This sacrament consists of something permanent from the moment of its consecration, the Real Presence.[19]

It is of faith that the whole and entire Christ is permanently contained under each species and in every part (at least that which is sensible, however small) separated from either species.[20] Thus, in every reception of the sacrament[21] the following *effects* may be received: 1) an increase in sanctifying or common or second grace, since the Eucharist is a sacrament of the living; 2) the special grace of this sacrament or sacramental grace, which consists in a spiritual nourishment through union with Christ and his members, thus accomplishing in the spiritual life what material nourishment or food and drink effects in bodily life, namely, sustaining, augmenting, repairing, delighting it; 3) a rich endowment of actual graces and a weakening of concupiscence and the inclination to sin even when habits have been formed; 4) the remission of venial sins and restoration of spiritual strength through the stirring up of charity in this sacrament whereby there is also a preservation from serious sins and all future sins; 5) a remission of the temporal punishment due to sin, not in whole but in part, according to the devotion and fervor of the recipient of the sacrament; 6) a pledge of future glory or consummated union with Christ in the beatific vision; 7) the remission of serious sins or the conferral of first grace, as an accidental effect of the sacrament and under the usual conditions.[22]

18. **Summa Theol.,** III, q. 73, a 4.
19. Jn. 6:52; c. 801; Trent, Denz.-Schön. 1636-1638; 1651-1652.
20. Trent, Denz.-Schön. 1653-1654; cf. S.C.D.F., 2 maii 1972, **de fragmentis eucharisticis;** cf. **Summa Theol.,** III, q. 76, aa. 2-3.
21. It is commonly taught that the reception of the Eucharist under both species imparts no increase of grace.
22. Cf. Jn. 6:48-59; I Cor. 10:16 sq.; Trent, Denz.-Schön. 1638; 1655; cf. **Summa Theol.,** III, q. 65, aa. 1, 3; q. 73, a. 1, ad 1; a. 3; q. 79.

THE EUCHARIST AS A SACRAMENT

II. Requirements for the Celebration of the Eucharist

A. *Requisite Material*

It is of faith that the requisite material of the sacrament of the Eucharist is wheaten bread and wine of the grape-vine[23] and not any substitute materials.

1. *Bread*

The bread must be made from wheat, mixed with natural water, baked by the application of fire heat (including electric cooking) and substantially uncorrupted.[24] The variety of the wheat or the region of its origin does not affect its validity, but bread made from any other grain is invalid material. Bread made with milk, wine, oil, etc., either entirely or in a notable part, is invalid material. Any natural water suffices for validity, e.g., even mineral water or sea water. The addition of a condiment, such as salt or sugar, is unlawful but valid, unless added in a notable quantity. Unbaked dough or dough fried in butter or cooked in water is invalid matter; likewise bread which is corrupted substantially, but not if it has merely begun to corrupt. Therefore, the valid material of this sacrament must be in the common estimation of reasonable men bread made from wheat and not mixed notably with something else so that it is no longer wheat.[25] Those who make altar breads must be satisfied that they have purchased genuine and pure wheat flour.

The bread must be of wheat *flour* and only in case of necessity a white material thrashed or crushed from wheat.[26] It must be free from mixture with any other substance besides wheat flour and water. It is gravely unlawful to consecrate with doubtful material. Altar breads must be fresh or recently baked and must

23. Florence, Denz.-Schön. 1320; c. 814.
24. c. 815, 1; **Missale Romanum** (1970), **Institutio Generalis,** ch. VI, nn. 281-283.
25. S.C. Sac. 26 mart. 1929.
26. S. Off. 23 iun. 1852.

not be allowed to get mouldy, which condition varies with regions, climates, etc. Normally the hosts should be renewed frequently;[27] to use a host more than a month old is generally unlawful, slightly or gravely depending upon the delay in renewal. No more hosts should be consecrated than can be consumed in suitable time. Breads should be clean and unbroken. To use a soiled or broken or disfigured host is slightly or seriously sinful depending upon the extent the host is affected or of the scandal that may arise.

In the Eastern Church the minister is gravely bound to use leavened bread (except the Armenians and Maronites who use un-leavened bread) ; Latin priests must use only unleavened bread.[28] A Latin may use leavened bread in the case of completing a eucha-ristic sacrifice already begun; likewise in an urgent case of pro-viding Viaticum.[29] Hosts must be round in shape in the Latin rite; in most Eastern rites they are square for the large host and tri-angular for the small breads. The large host usually carries on it the impression of the image of the Crucified.[30] Hosts for the Sacri-fice of the Mass should be larger than those for the communion of the faithful. If no large host is available, the celebrant may proceed with a small host, even in a Mass of private devotion, as long as no scandal is given. This procedure would be obligatory when there was need to consecrate for Viaticum or in order that people hear Mass on a day of precept.

2. *Wine*

To be valid material wine must be made from ripe grapes of the vine and not substantially corrupted;[31] it cannot come from any other fruits or from unripe grapes or from the stems and skins of the grapes after all the juice has been pressed out. In regions where fresh grapes cannot be obtained, it is lawful to use raisin wine, i.e., wine made by adding water to raisins.[32] Wine from

27. cc. 815; 1272; **Missale Romanum, loc. cit.,** n. 285.
28. Cf. Florence, Denz.-Schön. 1303; also c. 816; **Missale Romanum, loc. cit.,** n. 282.
29. Cf. cc. 851, 2; 866, 3.
30. S.C. Rit. 26 apr. 1834.
31. c. 815, 2; **Missale Romanum, loc. cit.,** nn. 284-285.
32. S. Off. 22 iul. 1706; 7 maii 1879; 10 apr. 1889.

which all alcohol has been removed or which on the other hand
has more than 20 per cent alcohol or to which foreign ingredients
(e.g., water) have been added in equal or greater quantities is
invalid material. Wine is likewise invalid which has turned to
acid or which is not natural but has been manufactured by some
chemical process, i.e., by mixing the constituents found in wine so
that the product resembles wine. Wine must also be in a potable
state, and thus if it is congealed (although most probably valid),
it must be melted. The color, strength or origin of wine does not
affect its validity.

It is gravely unlawful to use doubtful material and thus it is
unlawful to consecrate wine which is just beginning to turn sour
or to corrupt. Wine must be naturally fermented and the use of
"must" (unfermented grape juice) is gravely unlawful. To be lawful, wine must be pure, free from the lees, diseases, and foreign
ingredients. No addition may be made to wine except where the
Holy See[33] allows it, or where the addition is very small and a
just reason permits it. Lawful wine may not contain more than
18 percent alcohol (obtained from the grape); wines which would
not ordinarily ferment beyond 12 percent alcohol cannot be fortified
beyond this limit.[34] The Holy See has been insistent that sacramental
or Mass wine come from sources beyond suspicion, since there are
many ways in which wines can be vitiated or adulterated, many
methods which are actually used in this country to preserve, age,
ameliorate wines. Wine should never be purchased at a wine store
but only from reputable vendors of Mass wine with episcopal en-
dorsement.

It is a serious precept which requires that a very small portion
of water be mixed with the wine when about to be used in the
Holy Sacrifice.[35] This is not necessary by reason of the sacrament
but by ecclesiastical precept in order to signify that both water

33. **Ibid.,** 4 maii 1887; 30 iul. 1890; 15 apr. 1891; 27 apr. 1892; 9 maii
    1892; 22 mai 1901; 5 aug. 1906; 1 iun. 1910; 2 aug. 1922; 15 iul.
    1925; 16 dec. 1958; S.C. Sac. 26 mart. 1929.
34. S. Off. 5 aug. 1896.
35. c. 814; cf. Trent, Denz.-Schön. 1748; Florence, Denz.-Schön. 1320.

and blood issued from the side of the crucified Savior.[36] It is to be done at the prescribed time and before the offering of the wine. If the minister has forgotten to add the water, he should do so even after the Offertory, but never after the Consecration. If no water is available to mix with the wine to be consecrated at the Mass, theologians teach that a Mass is not to be celebrated or is to be interrupted, if begun, even though Viaticum is needed or the fulfillment of a precept (excepting proportionate scandal). The quantity to be added is usually three to ten drops. Priests should avoid too great concern over the exact number of drops. Even a single drop, as long as it is sensible, satisfies the precept; even one fifth water (or one fourth if the wine is stronger) is not unlawful, although an excess of one third the amount of wine renders the latter invalid or truly doubtful. If the quantity of water added appears to be more than lawful, the minister should add more wine or take fresh wine and add the correct amount of water.[37]

B. *Prescribed Words or Formula*

The formula of consecration of the bread is: "This is my body which will be given up for you"; of the wine: "This is the cup of my blood, the blood of the new and everlasting Covenant. It will be shed for you and for all men so that sins may be forgiven." (The word "*enim*" in the Latin formula does not pertain to validity and its omission is a slight sin.) The words which precede these formulas in no way pertain to the validity of the formula. It is commonly taught today that the essential words of the formula of the Eucharist—and their omission would invalidate the form—are: "This is my body," "This is the cup of my blood" (or "this is my blood"). In practice it is seriously prescribed to pronounce the

36. Cf. **Summa Theol.,** III, q. 74, a. 6.
37. If the priest notices after the consecration or when he receives Communion that water was poured into the chalice instead of wine, he is to pour the water into another container, then pour wine with water into the chalice and consecrate it. He says only the part of the narrative for the consecration of the chalice, without consecrating bread again (**Missale Romanum, Inst. Gen.,** n. 286).

entire formula; if any of the words from "the blood of the new. . ."
on are omitted, the whole formula is to be repeated conditionally.

The dignity of this sacrament wherein the priest speaks in the
person of Christ himself requires that the words of consecration
be spoken with the greatest care and reverence.[38] At the same time
they are to be said in a truly and normally human manner, without
scruples, as one speaks important words. The priest should not
interrupt the pronouncing of the formula nor repeat it nor bob his
head or move his body during its recitation; he would then represent Christ in a ridiculous manner and expose this most sacred
action to becoming a distraction to others or even displeasing.

All concelebrants at concelebrated Mass validly consecrate, even
if one accidentally finishes the form sooner than the others, the
recitation being considered morally simultaneous.[39] There is a
duty to repeat the formula only in a case of a serious and well-
founded and not scrupulous doubt. Repetition without a just reason
is in itself a serious sin, although a perplexed conscience may excuse. The minister should not be disturbed if he cannot recall
having said or said correctly the words required for consecration.
If the omission of some essential part is certain or doubtful, the
formula should be repeated absolutely or conditionally. If awareness
of the omission occurs at the consecration, the formula alone is
repeated; if later in the course of the Mass, the repetition begins
with the "The day before he suffered . . .", "Before he was given
up to death . . .", "On the night he was betrayed . . .", "He always
loved . . .", or with the "When supper was ended . . .", "In the same
way . . .", in the case of the formula of the wine alone.[40]

38. **Missale Romanum, Preces Eucharisticae,** nn. 91, 104, 111, 120.
39. On the other hand, S. Off. 23 maii 1957: "Q. Do several priests
validly concelebrate the Sacrifice of the Mass, if only one of
them pronounces the words 'Hoc est corpus meum' and
'Hic est sanguis meus' over the bread and wine, and the
others do not quote the words of the Lord, but, with the knowledge and consent of the celebrant, have and manifest the intention to make his words and actions their own. R. In the
negative, because, by the institution of Christ, he alone celebrates validly who pronounces the words of consecration."
40. **Missale Romanum, Preces Eucharisticae** I-IV.

C. *Physical Conjunction of Material and Formula*

The material for the Holy Sacrifice (and at the same time also for the confection of the sacrament) must be physically and morally present to the celebrant or minister who unites the matter with the form. This sacrament requires the maximum of presence and simultaneity of required material with prescribed formula so that the words *"this"* and *"this"* truly signify and are demonstrable. Thus, bread (host) which is on the corporal is present to the consecrator. It is not necessary that he see it, e.g., in a covered chalice or ciborium or in a group of hosts, but it is sufficient that it can be seen or touched in itself or in its container. A blind priest or one celebrating in darkness acts validly as long as he is morally certain of the presence of the required material.

Hosts located behind the altar or behind the priest, those locked in a tabernacle, those which are too far removed from the celebrant so as not to be designated by *"this"* but by *"that,"* e.g., more than fifty to a hundred feet away,[41] or material so small that it cannot be sensibly perceived, are not validly consecrated because not present. Hosts lying beneath the corporal or the altar cloth or the chalice, or behind the Missal, are doubtfully present. To leave the ciborium covered at the consecration is a slight sin, but it is validly consecrated. It suffices to incline slightly toward the bread and wine when pronouncing the formula of consecration.[42]

D. *Definite Intention*

The material to be consecrated must be *definitely* intended by the minister, since by intention the formula determines the significance of the material. Thus the material—and the question in practice offers some difficulty mostly in respect to the hosts—must be *determined* or *properly designated* by the minister's intention. Although an actual intention is preferred, at least a *virtual* intention

---

41. Cf. e.g., a concelebrated Mass. How near the hosts and wine must be to the celebrant to be morally present is left to the judgment of prudent men, the practice of the Church, the position and amount of the hosts and wine, etc.
42. **Missale Romanum,** loc. cit.

is required, which intention must be to consecrate the material or at least to do what the Church does.

The bread and wine to be consecrated should be placed on the corporal (or the altar cloth). If there is material to be consecrated or which is consecratable on the altar, but its presence is unknown to the celebrant, *by that very fact* it is not consecrated, since the intention of the minister must in *some sufficient* way designate or include the material that is to be consecrated.

The extent to which the celebrant understands material to be included in his intention, i.e., the meaning which the words *"this"* and *"this"* has for him in order to include all circumstances, can be determined by him once and for all, e.g., at the time of ordination, although it is recommended that this understanding in his own mind be renewed from time to time. On the other hand, his will to consecrate at any particular moment must be actual or at least virtual; unless changed, this will must be considered to be in conformity with his general or prevailing understanding of the terms of the intention. Every priest is urged in the beginning of his priesthood to form a clear intention regarding consecrating the sacred species and to recall it to mind in order to keep it fresh and to avoid anxiety and the danger of doubtful material.

By his intention the minister is considered to will (at least implicitly) to consecrate all that is before him, and thus he consecrates an unknown quantity of hosts in a ciborium or pyx or on the corporal or in his hands, e.g., if at the Communion he should notice that there have been two large hosts stuck together. Small particles remaining in the ciborium or pyx or on the corporal are considered to have been consecrated. Drops of wine adhering to the outside of the chalice are not considered to have been consecrated. Even though the interior surface of the chalice cup is wiped after the wine and water have been poured in for the Sacrifice, drops or a film of wine which sometimes nevertheless adhere to the sides of the cup are to be considered in practice to have been consecrated, since the intention of the minister is to consecrate all consecratable matter in the chalice.

Hosts which are doubtfully consecrated must not be administered to the faithful but rather reserved in the tabernacle and conditionally consecrated at another Mass; if they are few in number, they may be consumed at the same Mass but after the Sacred Blood has been consumed. Hosts which are to be consecrated are to be placed on the corporal (or the altar cloth) at the beginning of Mass, or at least before the Offertory. If for some reason they are brought out shortly after the Offertory, they are to be offered mentally. A serious reason is required if this takes place after the Preface has begun and a very serious reason after the Canon has begun. If one or another person would be deprived for some time of Holy Communion, a small particle from the large Mass host may be given. Under no circumstance may hosts be consecrated after the Mass host has been consecrated.

If consecrated hosts should become mixed with unconsecrated ones, the priest should consecrate the latter at a subsequent Mass and before being distributed to the faithful, either by consecrating the whole amount conditionally, or absolutely only those not consecrated. The same procedure is to be followed if a quantity of unconsecrated wine is added to render the Real Presence doubtful.

Even in a case of extreme necessity it is never allowed to consecrate except *within the Mass*.[43] A consecration which is not accompanied by the principal parts of the Mass is probably invalid. A consecration of one species alone is likewise gravely forbidden.[44] To consecrate one species without the intention to consecrate the other renders the consecration doubtful. If, however, the intention to consecrate the other does exist, the consecration is valid. Thus, in the case of the sudden incapacity of the celebrant, another priest can continue the liturgy of the Mass with the consecration of the other species.

III. Minister of Distribution

A. *Ordinary Minister*

It is certain teaching that the priest alone is the *ordinary* minister

43. c. 817.
44. **Ibid.**

of the distribution of Holy Communion.[45] However, any priest may distribute Communion during Mass, if he celebrates Mass privately (i.e., a low non-conventual Mass), also immediately before or immediately after Mass,[46] which he celebrates. Before Mass means after the priest has approached the altar for Mass; after Mass signifies before he leaves the altar after Mass. Even outside of Mass every priest has the right to administer Holy Communion with at least the presumed permission of the rector of the church.[47]

A priest with the care of souls has an obligation in justice to distribute Communion to his subjects whenever they reasonably request the same, unless he is lawfully impeded by a proportionate cause. He may fulfill his obligation by the ministrations of others. Other priests are bound in charity to minister the Eucharist to the dying, but not in other cases, since necessity is not considered to exist.

It is safe teaching in practice which allows a priest, a deacon, and others lawfully deputed to distribute Communion, to communicate himself outside of Mass (vested in surplice and stole), even out of devotion, but only in the circumstance that he cannot celebrate, that no other priest is available to administer to him, and that all scandal is avoided. A cleric or a layman may also communicate himself in order to avoid profanation of the Sacrament; it is probable that he may do the same when he is in danger of death and no priest is available. In certain sicknesses requiring special skill in the administration of Viaticum the priest may allow another, e.g., the Sister infirmarian, to administer the Eucharist, using a spoon or other instrument. Communion may be distributed at any Requiem Mass.

The right and duty of carrying Holy Communion publicly to the sick outside the church, even when they are not his parishioners, belongs to the pastor within his parish; other priests and deacons

---

45. c. 845, 1.
46. c. 846, 1. Cf. S.C.C.D., Instr. **Memoriale Domini** on the manner of distributing Communion, 29 maii 1969. The local Ordinary may for a just cause in a particular case forbid the distribution of Communion in a private oratory (c. 869).
47. c. 846,2.

can do so only in case of need or with the at least presumed permission of the pastor or local Ordinary.[48] To carry Holy Communion *publicly* is to observe the solemnities of the *Ritual;* to carry it *privately* is to wear a stole under the outer garment and to repose the Blessed Sacrament in a pyx which is carried with due reverence and decency.[49] Any priest or deacon can carry Holy Communion to the sick privately with at least the presumed permission of the priest to whom the custody of the Blessed Sacrament has been entrusted.[50]

The pastor has the exclusive right to bring Viaticum both publicly and privately to the sick in his parish, even to those not his parishioners.[51] Other priests can do this only in the case of need or with the at least presumed permission of the pastor or local Ordinary. The pastor's prerogative is restricted to the first administration of the Eucharist as Viaticum. The superior of a clerical religious house has this right over his own subjects and those staying in his house.[52] To the professed and the novices outside the house he can bring Viaticum privately or with the permission of the pastor publicly. Confessors of nuns with solemn vows enjoy this right, as also do chaplains of lay institutes whose house has been withdraw by the local Ordinary from the jurisdiction of the pastor.[53]

The liturgy prescribed for the distribution of Communion during Mass and outside of Mass, to the sick and to the dying, is to be observed by all. It is forbidden (in order to avoid false devotion) to give more than one particle to the same communicant or a larger host, whether out of devotion or any other reason.[54] A reasonable cause will excuse, e.g., if the priest cannot easily consume all the hosts that remain. If there are not enough hosts for the number of communicants, it is permissible to break each one

---

48. cc. 847; 848; 468, 1; 462, 2o; Paul VI, motu proprio **Ad pascendum,** 15 aug. 1972.
49. Cf. c. 849, 2.
50. c. 849, 1; motu proprio **Ad pascendum.**
51. cc. 850; 462, 3o.
52. c. 514, 1.
53. **Ibid.,** 2-3; the rector of a seminary has this right (c. 1368).
54. S.C. Conc. 12 feb. 1679.

into two or three parts.[55] Smaller divisions would be too small for sensible retention for the stomach. Particles which are left over should be consumed by the celebrant before the ablutions, if this can be easily done, or brought to another tabernacle, if they could not be otherwise consumed by celebrant or communicants. Holy Communion is to be distributed under the appearance of leavened or unleavened bread as the celebrant's rite requires, except in a case of urgent need and the unavailability of a priest of different rite, but always observing one's proper rite in the act of administration.[56]

B. *Extraordinary Minister*

1. *Deacon*

By ordination a *deacon* is the *extraordinary* minister of Holy Communion to be exercised with due permission of the local Ordinary or of the pastor, which permission may be presumed in a case of need.[57] Apart from necessity a deacon would not be justified in acting without permission. Examples of need are Viaticum for a sick person, the large number of communicants and the insufficiency of priests, etc. The required permission can be granted by the rector of a church, seminary rector, religious superior. Even with priests present a deacon may transfer the Blessed Sacrament from one altar to another.[58]

The deacon in administering Holy Communion observes the ceremonies as prescribed for a priest. He wears the stole in the fashion of a deacon and, unless a priest also distributes at the same time, he gives his blessing with his hand at the end of the

---

55. S.C. Rit., 16 mart. 1833.
56. c. 851.
57. c. 845, 2. **Lumen gentium, 29**: "It is the duty of the deacon to the extent that he has been authorized by competent authority . . . to be custodian and dispenser of the Eucharist." Cf. also Apostolic Letter **Sacrum Diaconatum Ordinem, 22** (18 iun. 1967); motu proprio **Ad pascendum.**
58. S.C. Rit. 23 nov. 1906.

ceremony as prescribed.[59] The deacon, although sinning gravely, does not incur an irregularity if he acts without permission.[60]

2. Others

The faculty may be given by the Holy See to local Ordinaries to permit suitable persons under their jurisdiction to administer Holy Communion to themselves and to the faithful.[61] The faculty may be used: a) whenever a priest or deacon is not available; b) whenever the usual minister is unable to administer Communion conveniently because of poor health, advanced age, or the demands of the pastoral ministry; c) whenever the number of the faithful who wish to receive Communion is so great that the celebration of Mass would be unduly prolonged.[62]

Suitable persons, in order of preference, are: canonically installed acolytes and lectors, men religious, women religious, male catechists (unless in the prudent judgment of the pastor a woman catechist is preferable), lay men, lay women.[63] Such persons are qualified by being chosen by name by the local Ordinary and receiving a mandate from him in accordance with the *Rite for Commissioning a Minister*.[64] Moreover, if he has received the faculty from the Holy See, the local Ordinary may permit priests with the care of souls to depute a suitable person, in the order of preference above, to distribute Communion on a particular occasion (*ad actum*) in cases of necessity and observing the *Rite for Deputing a Minister*.[65]

Local Ordinaries, who have received the faculty from the Holy See, may permit: a) men superiors who are not in sacred orders and women superiors and their substitutes to give Communion to themselves, to members of their communities, to the faithful who

59. PCI 13 iul. 1930.
60. Paul VI, motu proprio **Ministeria Quaedam,** VI (15 aug. 1972).
61. S.C. Sac. Instr. **Fidei custos,** 30 apr. 1969, cf. Instruction **Immensae Caritatis,** below, p. 193.
62. Ibid., n. 1; cf. **Immensae Caritatis.**
63. Ibid., n. 3; **Ministeria Quaedam,** whereby the ministries assume the functions of the subdiaconate; cf. **Immensae Caritatis.**
64. Ibid., n. 6; cf. **Immensae Caritatis.**
65. Ibid., n. 6a; cf. **Immensae Caritatis.**

may be present, and to the sick who live in their religious house; b) men superiors and rectors who are not in sacred orders and women superiors, as well as their substitutes, and any devout member of the faithful to give Communion to themselves, members of the institution (orphanage, hospital, college, other institution of any kind directed by religious), the faithful who are present, and to bring Communion to the sick.[66]

The local Ordinaries of the U.S.A. are authorized to permit: a) suitable persons to give Communion to themselves, distribute it to the faithful, and to bring it to the sick, in churches and public oratories, in the absence of an ordinary minister of Communion or if the latter is impeded by age, bad health, or the pastoral ministry; b) lay superiors of religious communities or those who take their place to give Communion to themselves and to distribute it to the members, the faithful who may be present, and the sick in the oratory of the religious house and in the same circumstances; c) suitable persons to assist the celebrating priest in the administration of Communion during Mass, in churches and public oratories, when a very lengthy distribution of Communion cannot otherwise be avoided. Priests having the time and opportunity are not thereby excused from distributing Communion to the faithful, especially the sick, when they legitimately request it.[67]

IV. Candidates for Eucharistic Communion

A. *Right to receive the Eucharist*

Baptism of water alone is the gateway to the other sacraments. Every baptized person who is not restrained by law can and should be admitted to Holy Communion.[68] It is unlawful to give Communion to a person in whom at least an habitual and implicit intention cannot be presumed, e.g., by his Christian manner of living.

66. **Ibid.,** n. 4; cf. **Immensae Caritatis.**
67. S.C. Sac. 18 iun. 1972; cf. **Immensae Caritatis.**
68. c. 853.

It is more common opinion that the grace of Holy Communion is received when the sacred species is received into the stomach. It is thus necessary to beware that the sacred species does not melt or corrupt in the mouth, especially because it is too small a particle, but is swallowed as soon as possible in order for it to reach the stomach since this sacrament is received after the manner of eating and drinking. If the recipient should die or vomit after the sacred species has been received in the stomach, the grace of the sacrament has been received. It is disputed whether the sacrament continues to confer grace as long as the species remain incorrupt in the stomach, given the fervor of charity in the well-disposed recipient, or confers the grace once and for all as a sacrament in the instant of eating or reception into the stomach. It is thus important that especially in its first reception the Holy Eucharist be most fervently received. It is commonly held as a norm that after Communion the Real Presence under the sensible species perdures for one-quarter hour after Communion, although this varies with the different conditions of each stomach.

Although the Eucharist as a sacrifice can benefit others inasmuch as it is offered for their salvation, it cannot, received as a *sacrament*, benefit others, since it is a spiritual food and drink which benefit only the partaker. However, Communion can benefit others as an act of satisfaction made to God for others, as suffrage for them, as quickening of charity which renders one more ready to petition God for others.[69]

B. *The Unprepared*

By divine law the Holy Eucharist should be withheld from one who in receiving it is likely, from his physical or mental condition, to cause irreverence.[70] It is unlawful to distribute Holy Communion

---

69. Cf. **Summa Theol.,** III, q. 79, a. 7.
70. In case of necessity, depending on the judgment of the Bishop, it is permitted to give the Eucharist under the species of wine alone to those who are unable to receive it under the species of bread. In this case it is permissible, with the consent of the local Ordinary, to celebrate Mass in the house of the sick person. If, however, Mass is not celebrated in the presence of the sick person, the Blood of the Lord should be kept in

to those who cannot distinguish ordinary bread from the Sacred Host due to lack of due reverence. Those who have never enjoyed the use of reason, since they are likened to infants, may not be given Communion even as Viaticum. Those who are insane, delirious or unconscious, if they had the use of reason and have lived a Christian life, can be presumed to possess a sufficient intention, but probably there will be danger of irreverence in the actual case. Viaticum can be given to those who in lucid intervals can absorb sufficient instruction to reverence the Real Presence.

Those who are subject to violent or fitful coughing or vomiting may not be given even Viaticum, unless there is a well-founded hope that between the spasms there is no danger of the Sacred Host being emitted. Medical advice on the recipient's condition may be consulted to ascertain whether the Communion will set off another seizure or whether It can be received or retained in the stomach. In danger of death it may be expedient to experiment first with a small amount of solid or liquid food.

C. *The Unworthy*

The unworthy are to be excluded from receiving Communion, i.e., public sinners such as those who are excommunicated, interdicted, notoriously infamous in law or fact, those living in concubinage or married outside the Church, members of a forbidden Society, those engaged in sinful occupation, unless their repentance and amendment is publicly known and the public scandal caused by them has been previously repaired.[71] Secret sinners who privately

a properly covered chalice and placed in the tabernacle after Mass. It should be taken to the sick person only if contained in a vessel which is closed in such a way as to eliminate all danger of spilling. When the sacrament is administered, that method should be chosen from the ones given in the **Ritus servandus in distributione communionis sub utraque specie** which is most suited to the case. When Communion has been given, should some of the Precious Blood still remain, it should be consumed by the minister; he will also carry out the usual ablutions (Instr. **Eucharisticum mysterium,** 41).

---

71. c. 855, 1. Included among the unworthy are truly and gravely immodestly dressed women and girls (S.C. Conc. 12 ian. 1930).

request Communion are to be refused if the priest knows that they have not repented; they may not be refused when they make the request publicly and the priest cannot disregard them without scandal.[72] Communion is likewise denied to one who clearly intends to dishonor the Sacred Host, even if he is a secret sinner publicly requesting Communion.

D. Non-Catholics

It is possible, and in certain respects desirable, for non-Catholics to receive the Eucharist in the Catholic Church. The *conditions* for inter-communion in particular cases are: 1) the recipients must have the same faith in the Eucharist as is professed by Catholics; 2) they must have a deep spiritual need for the Eucharist; 3) they must have been unable, over a prolonged period, to communicate in their own Church; 4) of their own accord they must request the Sacrament of Communion; 5) it is for the *local Ordinary* to make the decision in each case. In particular cases these conditions are more readily verifiable in the case of members of the separated Eastern Churches.[73] Where one of these conditions is lacking, admission to Eucharistic Communion in the Catholic Church is not possible.[74]

The celebration of the sacraments is an action of the celebrating community, carried out within the community, signifying the oneness in faith, worship, and life of the community. Where this unity of sacramental faith is deficient, the participation of the separated brethren with Catholics, especially in the sacraments of the Eucharist, Penance, and the Anointing of the Sick, is forbidden. Nevertheless, since the sacraments are both signs of unity and sources of grace, the Church can for adequate reasons allow access to those sacraments to a separated brother. This may be permitted in danger

---

72. **Ibid.,** 2.
73. Cf. Secr. ad unitatem Christianorum fovendam, 14 mai 1967, **Directorium,** 40, 42, 44, 50.
74. Secr. ad unitatem Christianorum fovendam, 7 ian 1970, Decl. **The Position of the Catholic Church in the matter of common Eucharist among Christians of different confessions,** 7; cf. Vatican II, Decrees **Orientalium Ecclesiarum,** 27; **Unitatis redintegratio,** 8, 15, 22.

of death or in urgent need (during persecution, in prisons) if the separated brother has no access to a minister of his own communion and spontaneously asks a Catholic priest for the sacraments—so long as he declares a faith in these sacraments in harmony with that of the Church, and is rightly disposed. In other cases the judge of this urgent necessity must be the diocesan bishop or the episcopal conference. A Catholic in similar circumstances may not ask for these sacraments except from a minister who has been validly ordained.[75]

Behind this teaching is the necessity to safeguard simultaneously the integrity of ecclesial communion and the good of souls. Two main governing ideas are: a) The strict relationship between the mystery of the Church and the mystery of the Eucharist can never be altered, whatever pastoral measures some may be led to take in given cases. Of its very nature celebration of the Eucharist signifies the fullness of profession of faith and the fullness of ecclesial communion. This principle must not be obscured and must remain the guide in this field. b) The principle will not be obscured if admission to Catholic Eucharistic communion is confined to particular cases of those Christians who have a faith in the sacrament in conformity with that of the Church, who experience a serious spiritual need for the Eucharistic sustenance, who for a prolonged period are unable to have recourse to a minister of their own community and who ask for the sacrament of their own accord: all this provided that they have proper dispositions and lead lives worthy of a Christian. This spiritual need should be understood in the sense of a need for an increase in spiritual life and a need for a deeper involvement in the mystery of the Church and its unity. Further, even if those conditions are fulfilled, it will be a pastoral responsibility to see that the admission of these other Christians

75. **Directorium,** 55; cf. also 6-7. Paul VI to members of the same Secretariate, 13 nov. 1968: "We need not tell you that, to promote ecumenism in an efficacious way, one must also guide it, submit it to rules that are quite precise. We regard the Ecumenical Directory not as a collection of advisory principles which one can freely accept or ignore, but as an authentic instruction, an exposition of the discipline to which all those who wish to truly serve ecumenism should submit themselves."

to Communion does not endanger or disturb the faith of Catholics.[76]

Different directives are laid down for the admission to Holy Communion of separated Eastern Christians and of others, because the Eastern Churches, though separated, have true sacraments and, above all, because of the apostolic succession, the priesthood, and the Eucharist which unite them to Catholic Christians by close ties, so that the risk of obscuring the relation between Eucharistic communion and ecclesial communion is somewhat reduced. But with Christians who belong to communities whose eucharistic faith differs from that of the Church and which do not have the sacrament of Orders, admitting them to the Eucharist entails the risk of obscuring the essential relation between Eucharistic communion and ecclesial communion. This is why their case differs from that of the Eastern Christians and envisages admission only in exceptional cases of urgent necessity and requires that they manifest a faith in the Eucharist as Christ instituted it and as the Catholic Church hands it down.[77]

Apart from circumstances of danger of death, prison confinement, and those suffering persecution, other cases of such urgent necessity need not be confined to situations of suffering and danger. Christians may find themselves in grave spiritual necessity and with no chance of recourse to their own community, such as with non-Catholics scattered in Catholic regions who are often deprived of the help of their own communion and unable to get in touch with it except at great trouble and expense. If the conditions prescribed are verified, they can be admitted to Eucharistic communion, but it will be for the *local Ordinary* to consider *each case*.[78]

V. Requirements for the Reception of the Eucharist

A. *Dispositions of Soul*

76. Secr. ad unitatem Christianorum fovendam, 1 iul. 1972, **Instruction concerning cases when other Christians may be admitted to Eucharistic Communion in the Catholic Church, 4.**
77. **Ibid., 5.**
78. **Ibid.**

1. *State of Grace*

The Eucharist is a sacrament of the living and thus is lawfully received only by those who are in the state of grace.[79] It is recommended that prayers of preparation and thanksgiving accompany the reception of the Eucharist, especially if outside of the Mass.[80]

No one with a serious sin on his conscience, no matter how contrite he may deem himself to be, is to approach Holy Communion without a previous sacramental confession of his sin; but in a case of urgent need and of the unavailability of a confessor, he is first to make an act of contrition.[81] For the reception of Communion, not absolute certainty but a prudent estimation is required that one is free from all serious sin. The obligation of confessing regards serious sins committed since the last worthy confession. Serious sins for which there was sorrow but which were forgotten in the last confession, or a state of serious doubt whether serious sin is present or not, do not oblige one to confess before going to Communion, although this is recommended, but renewal of perfect contrition suffices. Even when Communion is lawfully received without confession, the obligation remains of submitting to the keys all grave matter not directly remitted.

2. *Need of the Sacrament*

A need to celebrate or to communicate is present if Mass or Communion cannot be omitted without scandal, defamation of character or injury to another. A serious need to *celebrate* is, e.g.,: if Viaticum must be consecrated; if the priest must celebrate Mass for the people on a day of precept, on the occasion of a wedding, funeral, etc.; if he must satisfy an obligation assumed, e.g., a Gregorian series; if he remembers a serious sin after beginning Mass; if failure to say Mass would cause scandal or loss of reputation; if he must complete the unfinished Sacrifice of another celebrant. The purpose of hearing Mass himself, devotion to a certain feast, the gaining of a stipend, etc., are insufficient causes.

---

79. Cf. I Cor. 11:28.
80. Cf. Instr. **Eucharisticum mysterium,** 38.
81. c. 856.

A serious need to *communicate* is, e.g.,: if the Sacred Species must be protected from profanation by evil persons; if the communicant, already at the altar rail, remembers an unconfessed serious sin or when such a recollection befalls a member of a wedding party just before the ceremony when all are to receive Communion, etc. Devotion, the desire to satisfy one's Easter duty, etc., are not justifying reasons. A daily communicant in a group or in a community may not, when he is conscious of sin and has not already confessed it, make an act of perfect contrition and receive Communion, even though the abstention may cause some wonderment among others. Many reasons can be given—or should at least be understood by others as possible—which easily explain a failure to go to Communion.

3. *Freedom of Reception*

The Church has sought to provide in schools, seminaries, and religious communities a freedom to abstain as well as to communicate.[82] Opportunity for confession, especially before Communion, should be provided. The superior, while showing pleasure at frequent Communion, should likewise indicate no reproach for those who abstain. Superiors should take care that Communion is not brought to the sick who do not request it. The faithful are to be exhorted to practice daily reception of Communion but with the realization that this is not obligatory. If a term "general" Communion for the people is used, it should be clear to all that no one is obliged to receive on this occasion, and the approach to Communion should be in such a manner that no one is deterred from abstaining freely from the reception of Communion.

4. *Lack of an Available Confessor*

This refers, not to a lack of choice between confessors or to the absence of one's usual confessor, but to the absence of an approved confessor together with the inability to go to another without great difficulty, e.g., if a priest present were incapable or

---

82. S.C. Sac. 8 dec. 1938. Religious constitutions which may still provide for specified days for Communion are merely directive and not preceptive.

unwilling to hear the confession, as when the penitent is deaf, an accomplice, etc.; if an absent confessor cannot be reached without great difficulty, which is a relative inconvenience, such as one or two hours' journey; if the penitent fears that from confession a serious inconvenience will arise which is *extrinsic* to confession and excuses from material integrity. Any great difficulty or confusion, repugnance or embarrassment caused by confessing one's sins is *intrinsic* to the institution of confession and does not excuse from the obligation. Confession by its nature is not easy and its inconveniences have been made part of the sacrament. Some theologians maintain, and it is safe to hold in practice, that a penitent may be excused from this obligation (as though a confessor were lacking) when the difficulty in confessing to a particular confessor is truly extraordinary and almost insuperable with regard to certain serious sins that must be confessed, e.g., a sister to her brother, a mother to her son, etc.[83]

5. *Special Case of Priests*

A priest who is conscious of serious sin, no matter how contrite he may believe himself to be, should not dare to celebrate Mass without first receiving sacramental absolution; but if, lacking a confessor to whom he is obliged to confess and at the same time being bound by necessity to celebrate, he then celebrates after having made an act of perfect contrition, he must go to confession as soon as possible (*quam primum*).[84] The obligation of confessing as soon as possible after celebrating Mass is a serious precept[85] and the time is not left to the arbitrary decision of the priest. It is an obligation distinct from that of confessing before celebrating Mass. The confession must be made *within three days*, even if the priest is not going to celebrate during that time. He is obliged to confess immediately after celebrating if a confessor is then available and it is foreseen that one will not be available later within the three-day period. The priest may not celebrate again without confessing, unless the condition of necessity together with the lack of

83. Cf. **Summa Theol., Suppl.,** q. 8, a. 4, ad 6.
84. c. 807; Trent, Denz.-Schön. 1646-1647.
85. S. Off. 18 mart. 1666, Denz.-Schön. 2058-2059.

a confessor still endures. The obligation does not bind a priest who has celebrated sacrilegiously either because there was no need to celebrate or because he failed to avail himself of the opportunity of confession or failed to make an act of perfect contrition. The purpose of the obligation—to deter even from celebrating—would hardly be realizable in such a case.

B. *Dispositions of Body*

Reverence for the sacrament of the Holy Eucharist demands that the recipient of Communion be decently attired according to his means. Its suitableness is determined by the practice of good Catholics in the place and by any diocesan regulations that are laid down. Both in and out of the church men are to assist at sacred ceremonies with their heads uncovered, unless the approved usage of the people or particular circumstances require a different practice; women are to assist at them with head covered and dressed modestly, especially when they approach the holy table.[86] Truly immodestly dressed women and girls, such as to offer scandal to the faithful, are to be forbidden admission to Holy Communion as unworthy.[87] To deny the sacrament the attire must be truly and gravely immodest so as to offer scandal to the faithful. Attire which is out of order by defect or excess, but not gravely immodest, is to be called to the attention of the offending party, but Communion given. Deacons and priests communicating in the manner of the laity should wear a stole.

Cleanliness of body and/or attire befits the due reverence for this sacrament. A clean appearance should be presented and any bodily diseases, etc., which are notably disgusting, e.g, leprosy, advanced eczema, etc., as far as possible should be covered or Communion received privately or delayed until later. Marital intercourse when necessary or reasonable, menstruation, and involuntary pollution are not obstacles of themselves to the worthy reception of Communion.

86. c. 1262, 2; cf. Instr., S.C. Conc. 12 ian. 1930. It is fitting but not obligatory that the communicant divest himself of the weapons or arms he is wearing.
87. Cf. n. 71 above.

C. *Eucharistic Fast*

1. *Obligation*

Priests and faithful, before celebrating Holy Mass or receiving Holy Communion respectively, must for one hour abstain from solid foods and alcoholic liquids. Drinking water does not break the fast. The fast must be observed for the period of time indicated, which is to be estimated as one hour before the actual reception of Communion, for both priests and faithful.[88]

The precept to observe the eucharistic fast is a serious obligation founded in the tradition of the Church and based upon due reverence for the Blessed Sacrament. In the context of contemporary legislation very slight violations with regard to the quantity of food or drink or to the time element (unless done out of deliberate irreverence or of contempt) are not serious sins and thus of themselves do not preclude the reception of Communion.

A doubtful and not certain violation of the fast may be resolved in one's own favor, provided that there is no responsibility for the doubt because of a failure to ascertain the hour before deliberately eating and drinking in ignorance of the time.

Anything digestible taken into the stomach from the outside in the manner of eating or drinking, and not as saliva, by respiration or by injection, breaks the eucharistic fast.[89] What is solid food

---

88. Pius XII, Apost. Const. **Christus Dominus,** 6 ian. 1953; motu proprio **Sacram communionem,** 9 mart. 1957; S. Off. 10 ian. 1964; Paul VI, announcement, 21 nov. 1964; cf. S. Off. 18 iun. 1965. Cf. Instr. **Immensae Caritatis.**

89. The matter taken must come from outside; thus swallowing food which has previously lodged in the teeth or blood coming from the gums, etc., does not break the fast, but swallowing blood or skin from a finger does. There is no violation if things are taken into the mouth or tasted but then spit out again and not swallowed, e.g., to use tooth paste, to taste food in preparation, to chew tobacco (which is at least unbecoming before Communion). Chewing gum which is candy-coated breaks the fast but not ordinary chewing gum as long as the sugar or other element is absorbed into the saliva and then swallowed. There is no true eating if one unintentionally breathes in dust or an insect or snuffs in tobacco particles or nose drops. Smoking (even inhaling) is not a violation. Intra-

is left to the sound and common judgment of human association or the common estimation of prudent men. Solid food, whether hard or soft, is considered to be that which men are said to eat and with respect to the state in which it is when taken into the mouth, e.g., lozenges, pills, etc. Likewise with drink. It is considered to be that which men are commonly said to drink in the state in which it is taken into the mouth. The drink may be pure or it may be nutritious, i.e., drink into which nutritious materials are mixed, as long as these latter are so dissolved in the fluid material that the whole can be reasonably said to be fluid.[90]

Alcoholic drinks are those which are everywhere considered to be and are called alcoholic, e.g., wine, beer, whiskey, gin, rum, liqueurs, etc. A drink is alcoholic whether taken by itself or mixed with something else, no matter how small the quantity of alcohol. Medicine is that which is so considered in the sound and common judgment of men. Common consent generally regards medicine prescribed by a physician as true and proper medicine. In a case of doubt whether a thing is true and proper medicine a sound and present judgment, based on solid and positive probability, may be followed. In fact, where there is a consideration of true and proper medicines, even if they contain alcohol, as long as they qualify as true and proper

venous feeding does not break the fast nor a small amount of lubrication which may remain after a stomach lotion. The following are not considered as digestible (at least probably) and thus do not break the fast: hair, sand, dirt, chalk, glass, iron, wood, silk, wool, paper, wax, straw, fingernails, etc.

90. Alfred Cardinal Ottaviani, Pro-Secretary of the Holy Office (**Oss. Rom.,** 23 mart. 1957): "After the promulgation of the Motu Proprio, **Sacram Communionem,** the following questions have been proposed to the Holy Office and to Ordinaries or have been discussed in periodicals: . . . 2. Could one consider as liquid a solid, e.g., a sweet, which will dissolve in the mouth before it is swallowed? R. In the negative; it must already be liquid before it is put into the mouth." S. Off. 7 sept. 1897: "The mind (of the Congregation) is that when the expression '**per modum potus**' is used, it is understood that the person may take broth, coffee, or other liquid food, in which is mixed some substance such as wheat meal, grated bread, and the like, provided the whole mixture continues to have the nature of liquid food."

medicines in the commonly accepted sense of the word, they may be taken by the sick without any limitation of time whatsoever.[91]

2. *Special Circumstances*

All priests who are going to celebrate Mass twice or more times may in the prior Masses take two ablutions as noted in the rubrics of the Missal, but using only water. But if a priest who must celebrate a Mass a second or more times inadvertently takes wine also, in the ablution, he is not prohibited from celebrating the subsequent second or more Masses.[92]

The local Ordinary may permit priests who celebrate two or three Masses to take something by way of drink even though an interval of one hour does not intervene before the celebration of the next Mass.[93] This very probably excludes alcoholic drink. This faculty may be used even before the first of the series of Masses.

In a case of danger (even probable) of death from any cause, whether internally or from without, one may receive Communion (especially as Viaticum) even daily without fasting.[94] Likewise a priest may celebrate Mass without fasting when it is necessary to provide Viaticum.

One may consume the Blessed Sacrament without fasting when there is need to safeguard it from irreverence or profanation, e.g., by desecrators, by fire or flood, bombs, etc.[95] Likewise when the celebrant discovers particles remaining after his Mass, or when he has become aware of consuming invalid matter and he must consecrate new matter. If the celebrant after the consecration remembers that he has not been fasting, he must continue with the Communion. If he finds that he is unable to continue after the consecration, even a priest who is not fasting must complete the Sacrifice.

A truly serious inconvenience may excuse from the obligation of the eucharistic fast. Thus, in order to avoid scandal or defamation in a case in which the eucharistic fast is inadvertently broken,

91. Cardinal Ottaviani, **loc. cit.**
92. **Christus Dominus,** 7-8.
93. Motu proprio **Pastorale munus,** 30 nov. 1963, I, n. 2.
94. Cf. c. 858, 1; Also Instr. **Immensae Caritatis.**
95. **Ibid.**

a candidate may receive Communion in the Mass accompanying the reception of Orders, a priest may proceed to celebrate his first Mass, and a person at the altar rail or a child before First Communion remembering having broken the fast may receive Communion. A priest who has broken his fast by taking solid food or drink (as distinct from the question of ablutions and excepting the faculty to do so granted by the local Ordinary), may not celebrate a second Mass that day,[96] or even any Mass if he is not fasting as prescribed. However, he may celebrate if this is necessary for the people to satisfy their precept of hearing Mass since usually offense is given to the people and the majority would not assist at Mass elsewhere. It is likewise possible that he may celebrate Mass without fasting even on another day if circumstances so conspire that infamy or scandal or great damage would arise from the omission of the Mass that day, e.g., a funeral or wedding.

The infirm, even though not confined to bed, can take non-alcoholic drink and true and proper medicines, either liquid or solid, without limitation of time, before celebrating Mass or receiving Holy Communion. In some cases a eucharistic fast from food and alcoholic drink is permitted for only one quarter of an hour.[97]

Infirmity in the wide sense of the word is the weakening or the deficiency or the absence of health and thus is much broader than

96. S. Off. 2 dec. 1874: "Q. Whether by reason of scandal or astonishment one can ever celebrate the second Mass after the first when the fast has already been broken. R. In the negative." A priest who celebrates without fasting may be suspended (c. 2321).
97. **Sacram communionem**, 2. S. Off. 21 oct. 1961: "Q. Whether it is permitted to administer Holy Communion in the afternoon hours to the infirm, even though they are not in danger of death nor confined to bed but are unable to leave the house, as often as they have not been able to receive the Holy Eucharist in the morning, either due to the absence of a priest, or for some other reasonable impediment. R. Affirmative, as long as: 1) it is a question of the infirm who now for a week have not been able to leave the house; 2) the time and frequency of Holy Communion are determined by the pastor or another priest to whom the spiritual care of the infirm party is entrusted; 3) the rules already established for the eucharistic fast are observed." Cf. Instr. **Immensae Caritatis.**

the notion of sickness or disease. In the context of the eucharistic fast the notion of infirmity is based upon the sound and common estimation of men, who in their well-balanced judgment do not regard every indisposition or weakness as infirmity. Infirmity may be serious or light, chronic or acute, passing or enduring, requiring confinement or not, painful or painless, evident or hidden, more or less somatic or psychic, etc. In a case of doubt an indisposition or weakening of strength can be regarded as an infirmity. It suffices that a person of sound judgment and right conscience judges with true and positive probability that the particular case verifies the notion of infirmity.

D. *Frequency of Reception*

No one is permitted to receive the Holy Eucharist again if he has already received it on the same day, unless specifically authorized.[98] However, if he should fall into the danger of death or if there is a need to prevent irreverence to the Sacrament, he may and even must communicate again.[99]

Sacred ministers who perform their function in concelebrated Masses twice on the same day may also receive Communion under both species twice on the same day.[100] If any priest acts as a ministering deacon, assistant deacon, or subdeacon in a concelebrated Mass, he is not to concelebrate in that Mass. However, the deacon, subdeacon, and assistant deacons may receive Communion under both kinds. If they are priests, moreover, they may receive in this fashion even if they have already celebrated Mass or are to celebrate Mass.[101]

At the conventual Mass in religious communities members of the community who are priests and who are bound to celebrate individually may communicate under both kinds.[102]

The faithful who begin to celebrate the Sunday or holy day of

---

98. c. 857. S.C. Sac. 16 oct. 1972. Cf. Instr. **Immensae Caritatis.**
99. cc. 858, 1; 864.
100. Conc. Com. Lit., mai 1965.
101. **Ibid., Ritus servandus in concelebratione Missae et Ritus communionis sub utraque specie,** 7 mart. 1965.
102. **Missale Romanum, Inst. Gen.,** 76.

obligation on the preceding evening may go to Communion at that
Mass even if they have already received Communion in the morning.[103] Those who have received Communion during the Mass of
the Easter Vigil or during the Mass of Christmas may receive Communion again at the second Easter Mass and at one of the Masses
on Christmas Day.[104] The priest who does not celebrate but only
communicates at these Masses may celebrate one or more Masses
the next day. The faithful who go to Communion at the Mass of
the Chrism on Holy Thursday may receive Communion again at
the evening Mass of the same day.[105]

VI. Obligation to Receive the Eucharist

A. *General Precept*

The actual reception of the Eucharist is strictly obligatory by
a necessity of precept for all who have reached the use of reason.[106]
By divine precept Communion must be received by those who are
in danger of or at the moment of death; moreover, the faithful
are likewise bound to refresh their souls with this heavenly bread
at some time during life. When and how often this precept binds
has been left for the Church to determine.

By ecclesiastical precept Communion must be received once
a year, at least during Paschaltide[107] and as often as it is required
in order to satisfy another precept, e.g., the reception of Orders.
A sacrilegious Communion does not satisfy either the divine or the
ecclesiastical precept.[108] The dispositions requisite for receiving
Holy Communion are a right intention and the state of grace.[109]

The faithful are to be exhorted to refresh themselves frequently,

---

103. Instr. **Eucharisticum mysterium,** 28.
104. S.C. Rit., 26 sept. 1964, Instr. **Inter oecumenici,** 60.
105. S.C. Rit., 4 maii 1967, Instr. **Tres abhinc annos,** 14.
106. Jn. 6:54; cf. Trent, Denz.-Schön. 1638; 1659; 1730; 1734.
107. c. 859, 1.
108. c. 861.
109. S.C. Conc. 20 dec. 1905. Cf. c. 856.

even daily, with the Eucharistic bread in accordance with the norms laid down in the decrees of the Apostolic See; and that those who assist at Mass receive Communion not only by a spiritual desire but also by the sacramental reception of the Holy Eucharist.[110]

Moreover, it is clear that the frequent or daily reception of the Blessed Eucharist increases union with Christ, nourishes the spiritual life more abundantly, strengthens the soul in virtue, and gives the communicant a stronger pledge of eternal happiness; therefore, parish priests, confessors, and preachers will frequently and zealously exhort the Christian people to this holy and salutary practice.[111] The Eucharist should be presented to the faithful as a medicine by which we are freed from our daily faults and preserved from serious sin.[112]

It is fitting to provide the nourishment of the Eucharist for those who are prevented from attending its celebration in the community. They will thus feel themselves united to this community and sustained by the love of their brethren. Pastors of souls are to take every care to make it possible for the sick and the aged to receive the Eucharist frequently, even if they are not gravely ill or in danger of death. In fact, if possible this could be done every day, and should be done in paschal time especially. Communion may be taken to such people at any time of the day.[113]

B. *First Communion*

The Eucharist should not be administered to children who, because of lack of age, do not have the knowledge or the intention required for the reception of this sacrament.[114] Children in danger of death are to be given Communion if they are able to distinguish between the Blessed Sacrament and ordinary bread, and if there is no danger of irreverence.[115] Though the fact may be otherwise

110. c. 863.
111. Instr. **Eucharisticum mysterium,** 37.
112. **Ibid.,** 35.
113. **Ibid.,** 40.
114. c. 854, 1.
115. **Ibid.,** 2.

in a particular case, it is presumed that a child does not have the requisite knowledge before the age of seven years.[116] Outside the danger of death a more thorough knowledge of Christian doctrine and a more detailed preparation are demanded, viz., that by which they may, in the degree in which they are capable, know at least the mysteries of the faith the knowledge of which is necessary for salvation and by which, when they approach the Blessed Sacrament, they may possess the devotion that is appropriate to their age.[117]

The obligation of the precept of receiving Communion binding on children under the age of puberty affects also and principally those who are charged with their care, i.e., their parents, guardians, confessors, teachers, and pastors.[118] This is a grave duty. When the child begins to use his reason the pastor has an obligation to see that he is admitted to Holy Communion, and the child is thenceforward obliged to receive it annually. Judgment in this matter belongs in the first place to the child's confessor, then to his parents and guardians. Pastors have the duty to see to it that children receive Communion as soon as possible, but not before they reach the use of reason or before they are properly prepared; if necessary they may assure themselves of this by an examination.[119] The admission of children to Communion is not a pastoral right, except in the absence of the confessor's decision or when he has a reasonable doubt regarding the child's present disposition.

The Holy See judges that the practice now in force in the Church of putting Confession ahead of first Communion should be retained.[120]

---

116. c. 88, 3; PCI 24 feb. 1920: "Q. Is the use of reason mentioned in c. 854, 2, 3, and 5; 859, 1, and 906 that required for the commission of a mortal sin or that sufficient for the commission of only a venial sin. R. The use of reason for Holy Communion is that clearly indicated in c. 854, 2, 3; for the precept of annual confession it is that indicated in c. 906."
117. c. 854, 3.
118. c. 860.
119. c. 854, 4-5.
120. S.C. pro Clero, 11 apr. 1971, **Directorium Catechisticum Generale, Addendum,** n. 5.

C. Easter Duty

1. Obligation

Everyone of the faithful of both sexes is bound, after he has reached the years of discretion, to receive the sacrament of the Eucharist once a year, at least at Easter, unless perchance with the advice of his own priest, for some justifying reason, he is convinced that he should temporarily abstain from reception of the sacrament.[121] This grave precept of annual Communion remains in force even after the Easter season has closed, but not as the precept of the Easter duty.[122] The more common reckoning is made from Easter to Easter, although the civil or liturgical year may be used, as long as more than a year in the terms of the law does not expire. The determination of the Easter season is not to remove the fulfillment of the obligation at another time but to urge the duty. It is commonly considered that children are bound by this precept only with the beginning of the Easter season which follows upon their attainment of the use of reason. They are bound even before they reach the age of seven if they have been admitted to First Communion because they were judged to possess the required discretion.[123]

2. Time

The common law requires that the Easter Communion be received between Palm Sunday and Low Sunday,[124] but an indult for the U.S.A. extends the period for fulfillment from the first Sunday of Lent until Trinity Sunday inclusively.[125] A person who foresees that he will not be able to communicate during the Easter season is obliged to anticipate the reception only if he will probably pass a whole year without having received Communion. This is

---

121. c. 859, 1; cf. Lateran IV, Denz.-Schön. 812; Trent, Denz.-Schön 1659.
122. **Ibid.,** 4.
123. PCI 3 ian. 1918; this also includes confession.
124. c. 859, 2.
125. Pius VIII, 26 sept. 1830; cf. II Baltimore, no. 257.

in order to satisfy the duty of annual Communion and not the Paschal precept, which does not yet oblige. The sick who have received Viaticum must nevertheless make their Easter duty. The pastor or confessor can declare that in particular circumstances there is a reasonable cause for an individual to defer the fulfillment of the precept for a time,[126] e.g., when absolution must be deferred until certain conditions are satisfied.

3. *Place*

The faithful are to be persuaded to satisfy their obligation in their own respective parishes; if anyone fulfills it in another parish he is to take care to inform his own pastor of this fact.[127] This is not an obligation, but only a counsel regarding the place and the report.

4. *Rite*

All the faithful of every rite are authorized, for the purpose of devotion, to receive the Sacrament in whatever rite it has been consecrated; it is desirable, however, that each one satisfy his Easter duty in his own rite.[128]

D. *Holy Viaticum*

Communion given as Viaticum should be considered as a special sign of participation in the mystery celebrated in the Mass, the mystery of the death of the Lord and his passage to the Father. By it, strengthened by the Body of Christ, the Christian is endowed with the pledge of the resurrection in his passage from this life.[129]

In danger of death from whatever cause it may arise the faithful are bound by the precept of Holy Communion.[130] The divine precept

---

126. c. 859, 1.
127. **Ibid.,** 3.
128. c. 866, 1-2.
129. Instr. **Eucharisticum mysterium,** 39.
130. c. 864, 1. The cause of death may be internal, e.g., disease, or external, e.g., those condemned to be beheaded (S.C. Sac. 11 feb. 1915; S.C.P.F. 21 iul. and 10 aug. 1841).

begins to bind as soon as there is some certainty of the actual presence of the danger (and not necessarily the imminence) of death; it ceases when the danger passes, even though Viaticum was not received. Viaticum is probably not obligatory if Communion has been received within eight days of the time of the presence of the mortal danger. However, it is strongly recommended that, even if the dying person received Communion on the same day before he was stricken, he should receive it again but as Holy Viaticum.[131] During the same danger of death Viaticum, according to the counsel of a prudent confessor, may be and is fittingly administered several times on distinct (and not the same) days,[132] even on successive days.

Pastors, also religious superiors, confessors, parents, etc., must ensure that the administration of this sacrament to the sick is not delayed but that they are nourished by it while still in full possession of their senses.[133] If the danger is not imminent, two or three days is not too long. Viaticum is to be given to dying children who can distinguish the Body of Christ from ordinary bread, even if they have not made their First Communion.[134] It is not to be administered to those who are continually subject to vomiting, coughing, etc., unless it is morally certain that the Host will not be expelled. It can probably be given to a person who has an artificial esophagus or to one who is fed through a stomach tube. In case of necessity Viaticum may be received in another rite.[135] Also, in case of necessity, depending on the judgment of the bishop, it is permitted to give the Eucharist under the species of wine alone to those who are unable to receive it under the species of bread.[136]

---

131. **Ibid.,** 2; Instr. **Eucharisticum mysterium,** 39.
132. **Ibid.,** 3.
133. c. 865; Instr. **Eucharisticum mysterium, loc. cit.**
134. S.C. Sac. 8 aug. 1910. Also Penance, Confirmation, the Last Anointing, and the Last Blessing should be given as provided in the liturgical norms and according to circumstances. Cf. S.C.C.D., 7 dec. 1972, **Ordo unctionis infirmorum eorumque pastoralis curae** (treated in **The Celebration of the Anointing of the Sick**).
135. c. 866, 3.
136. Instr. **Eucharisticum mysterium,** 41.

VII. Distribution of Holy Communion

A. *Place*

The celebrant of Mass is not permitted to distribute Communion to the faithful so distant that he loses sight of the altar,[137] i.e., outside the oratory or place of celebration and not including the obstructions in the place itself. Outside of Mass Communion may be distributed wherever it is permitted to celebrate Mass, even in a private oratory, unless forbidden by the local Ordinary.[138] In private homes the local Ordinary, and the religious Ordinary in his house, may permit distribution to those who are not sick but in an extraordinary and single case,[139] which faculty may be delegated.

B. *Time*

It is lawful to distribute Communion on all days.[140] Except for Viaticum,[141] Communion may be distributed only at those hours in which the Sacrifice of the Mass can be offered, unless a reasonable cause warrants otherwise.[142] The faithful should be accustomed to receive Communion during the actual celebration of the Eucharist. Even outside the Mass, however, priests should not refuse to distribute Communion to those who have good reason to ask for it.[143]

The local Ordinary may permit priests, for a just cause, to distribute Communion in the evening.[144] The major superior of a religious institute may permit, in his own houses, Communion to be distributed at any hour of the day for the good of the religious and for a just cause.[145]

The proper time for distributing Holy Communion to the faithful

137. c. 868.
138. c. 869.
139. c. 822, 4. Cf. S.C.C.D. **Instruction on Masses for Special Gatherings,** 15 maii 1969; also S.C. Rit. Declaration, 29 dec. 1966.
140. c. 667, 1. Cf. c. 857.
141. c. 867, 5.
142. **Ibid.,** 4.
143. Instr. **Eucharisticum mysterium,** 33.
144. Motu proprio **Pastorale munus,** I, 4.
145. Pont. Rescript, **Cum admotae,** 6 nov. 1964, I, 1.

is within the Mass, after the Communion of the celebrating priest, who himself distributes it to those who seek it, unless it is appropriate by reason of the great number of communicants that he be helped by another priest or priests. It is altogether improper, however, that Holy Communion be distributed by another priest, outside of the proper time of Communion, at the same altar at which the Mass is being celebrated.[146]

C. *Manner*

When Communion is distributed apart from Mass the priest must dress in surplice and stole of the color of the office of the day, or in a white stole (but not black or purple except the latter on All Souls' Day). To distribute Communion without any sacred vestment is a serious sin, without surplice or stole a slight sin, unless necessity excuses. There is a light obligation to use a corporal and to light two candles. Distribution is made with the thumb and first finger of the right hand, unless a reasonable cause in a particular instance should require other fingers. Although valid, it is an abuse and not lawful for another priest to distribute hosts immediately after their consecration and before the celebrant's Communion, except for the gravest causes, e.g., for Viaticum.[147]

In hospitals consisting of a single building in which there is a chapel, the priest is to recite in the chapel itself all the prayers which according to the Roman Ritual are to be said before and after the Communion of the sick and is to distribute the Eucharist to each of the sick persons in their respective rooms, using the formula of Communion. In hospitals consisting of more than one building, the Eucharist is to be reverently brought from the chapel and deposited on a table prepared in a decent and suitable place in each building and there, reciting the prayers that are to be said

---

146. John XXIII, motu proprio **Rubricarum instructum,** S.C. Rit. decree, 26 iul. 1960, n. 502, which continues: "On the other hand, it is also permissible for a good reason to distribute Holy Communion immediately before or after Mass, or even outside the time of Mass. In such cases the form prescribed in the **Roman Ritual,** tit. V. c. 2, nos. 1-10, is used."
147. S.C. Rit. 11 maii 1878.

before and after the Communion of the sick, the priest is to give Communion in the above manner.[148]

In accordance with the custom of the Church, Communion may be distributed to the faithful either kneeling or standing. One or the other way is to be chosen, *according to the decision of the episcopal conference*. When the faithful communicate kneeling, no other sign of reverence toward the Blessed Sacrament is required, since kneeling is itself a sign of adoration. When they receive standing, it is strongly recommended that, coming up in procession, at the right time and place they make a sign of reverence before receiving Communion, so that the order of people passing back and forth be not disrupted.[149]

D. *Under Both Species*

Holy Communion, considered as a sign, has a fuller form when it is received under both kinds. For under the form of both kinds the sign of the Eucharistic banquet appears more perfectly.[150] Moreover, it is more clearly shown how the new and eternal Covenant is ratified in the Blood of the Lord, as it also expresses the relation of the Eucharistic banquet to the eschatological banquet in the kingdom of the Father.[151]

Communion under both kinds may be distributed, in accordance with the judgment of the Ordinary, in the cases determined by the Holy See. The Episcopal Conference may decide to what extent, for what motives and in what conditions, Ordinaries may concede Communion under both kinds in other cases which have great importance for the spiritual life of a particular community or group of the faithful.[152]

148. S.C. Rit. Decree, 14 feb. 1966.
149. Instr. **Eucharisticum mysterium,** 34.
150. This leaves intact the principles of the Council of Trent by which under either species or kind there is received the true sacrament and Christ whole and entire (Denz.-Schön. 1726-1729).
151. Instr. **Eucharisticum mysterium,** 32.
152. S.C.C.D., Instr. **Sacramentali Communione,** 29 iun. 1970, 1-2. Ordinaries should not grant permission in particular cases on occasions when there are large numbers of communicants.

That method of distribution should be chosen which best ensures that Communion is received with devotion and dignity and also avoids the dangers of irreverence. The nature of each liturgical group, and the age, conditions, and preparation of those wishing to receive Communion must also be taken into account.

Among the ways of distribution the reception of Communion by drinking from the chalice itself certainly has preeminence. However, this method should only be chosen when everything can be carried out in an orderly fashion and without any danger of irreverence toward the Blood of the Lord. If there are other priests present, or deacons or acolytes, they should therefore, be asked to help by presenting the chalice. On the other hand, it does not seem that manner of distribution should be approved in which the chalice is passed from one to another, or in which the communicants come up directly to take the chalice themselves and receive the Blood of the Lord. When the above-mentioned ministers are not available, then if the communicants are few in number and Communion is taken directly from the chalice, the same priest should distribute Communion first under the species of bread and afterwards under the species of wine.

Otherwise, the rite of Communion under both kinds by intinction is to be preferred in order that practical difficulties may be avoided and that due reverence might be more aptly given to the Sacrament. In this way access to Communion under both kinds is offered more easily and more safely to the faithful, whatever their age or condition, and at the same time the fulness of sign is preserved.[153]

In accordance with the judgment of the Ordinary and after the necessary explanation, Communion from the chalice is permitted for the following:

1. adults at the Mass which follows their Baptism; adults at the Mass in which they are confirmed; the baptized who are being received into Communion with the church;

   Moreover, they should ensure the observance of the prescribed norms and rite as described in nn. 244-251 of the General Instruction in the **Missale Romanum** (ibid., 3-6).

---

153. **Ibid.,** 6.

2. the bride and bridegroom at their wedding Mass;
3. the newly ordained at their ordination Mass;
4. an abbess at the Mass in which she is blessed; virgins at the Mass of their consecration; professed religious, together with their parents, relatives, and members of their community, at the Mass during which they make or renew their vows of first or perpetual profession;
5. lay missionaries and others at the Mass in which they receive publicly an ecclesiastical mission;
6. the sick person and those present when Viaticum is administered at a Mass lawfully celebrated in the home of a sick person;
7. the deacon, subdeacon, and ministers who exercise their office at a Mass with singing;
8. when there is a concelebrated Mass:
   (a) all, including the laity, who exercise a genuine liturgical function in the concelebration and also all seminarians who are present;
   (b) in their churches and oratories, all members of institutes which practice the evangelical counsels and other societies whose members dedicate themselves to God by religious vows, offering, or promise, as well as all those who live day and night in the houses of such institutes and societies;
9. priests who are present at large celebrations and are not able to celebrate or concelebrate;
10. all who make a retreat or spiritual exercise, at a Mass specially celebrated for the participating group; all who take part in a meeting of a pastoral commission, at a Mass celebrated in common;
11. those listed in nos. 2 and 4 at their jubilee Masses; godparents, parents, and wife or husband of a newly baptized adult, and lay catechists at the Mass of initiation;
13. parents, relatives, and special benefactors who participate in the Mass of a newly-ordained priest;

14. members of communities at the conventual or community Mass.[154]

In the dioceses of the United States Communion from the chalice is permitted also for:[155]

1. other members of the faithful present on the special occasions enumerated in no. 242 of the General Instruction of the Roman Missal (above) ;
2. at funeral Masses and at Masses for a special family observance;
3. at Masses on days of special religious or civil significance for the people of the United States;
4. at Masses on Holy Thursday and at the Mass of the Easter Vigil, the norms of the Instruction of June 29, 1970, being observed;
5. at weekday Masses.

VIII. Custody of the Holy Eucharist

A. *Lawfulness*

The Blessed Sacrament has customarily been reserved since ancient times primarily to provide Viaticum for those in danger of death, but also as an opportunity for the faithful to communicate even outside of Mass and to foster the practice of visits to the Blessed Sacrament enclosed in the tabernacle.[156]

For the reservation of the sacred species for the sick led to the praiseworthy custom of adoring the heavenly food which is preserved in churches. This practice of adoration has a valid and firm foundation, especially since belief in the real presence of the Lord

---

154. **Ibid.,** appendix; **Missale Romanum, Instr. Gen.,** 242.
155. NCCB, 18 nov. 1970.
156. Cf. Trent, Denz.-Schön. 1645; Instr. **Eucharisticum mysterium,** 49.

has its natural consequence in the external and public manifestation of that belief.[157]

Two necessary conditions are required for reservation, viz., that there be a person charged with the custody of the tabernacle (even a layman), and that a priest regularly celebrates Mass at least once a week in the sacred place.[158] An omission of one or another week for a just cause does not seem to be a violation.

B. *Place of Reservation*

1. *Church*

The Eucharist must be reserved in a cathedral church or its substitute, in every parish or quasi-parish church, and in a church attached to a house of religious men or women.[159] Subsidiary and not strictly parochial churches are not so obliged but the local Ordinary may grant this permission.[160] The church or public oratory[161] of exempt religious whose house is lawfully erected must reserve the Eucharist. The church must serve the religious in their practice of divine worship (whether or not they have possession of the church), or the community must say its obligatory prayers in it, whether it is immediately joined to the religious house or not. Collegiate churches and the principal oratory, whether public or semipublic, of a pious or a religious house or an ecclesiastical college in charge of either priests or religious may be permitted by the local Ordinary to reserve the Eucharist.[162]

---

157. Instr. **Eucharisticum mysterium, loc. cit.**
158. c. 1265, 1.
159. **Ibid.,** 1o. Such churches should remain open at some times for the faithful (c. 1266).
160. PCI 20 maii 1923.
161. c. 1191, 1.
162. c. 1265, 1. 2o; and only in the church or principal oratory. Ecclesiastical colleges are minor and major seminaries, juniorates, scholasticates, religious novitiates. Even clerical exempt religious need permission of the local Ordinary for such reservation in the oratories of their pious or religious houses and ecclesiastical colleges. A pious house is one the spiritual needs of which are provided for by a chaplain and which is devoted, from a supernatural motive and under ecclesiastical control, to the promotion of religion or charity,

The Eucharist may be reserved in another place in the same building if there exist groups so distinct from one another as to constitute separate houses of religious or piety.[163] An Apostolic indult is needed for reservation in other churches or oratories. The local Ordinary can also permit this for a justifying reason and for a given occasion (*per modum actus*), but only for a church or a public oratory,[164] which permission may be not granted habitually (*pro semper*) but it may endure for the length of the justifying cause, e.g., during repair work. No one is allowed to keep the Blessed Sacrament in his house or to carry it with him while traveling.[165] If a serious reason, approved by the local Ordinary, warrants it, it is not forbidden to keep the Blessed Sacrament outside the tabernacle, but only at night and on a corporal in a safe and worthy place with a lamp burning. This is usually a safe in the sacristy, or even some private place if necessary, with all due reverence.[166]

2. Tabernacle

Where the reservation of the Blessed Sacrament is permitted according to the provisions of law, it may be reserved permanently or regularly only on one altar or in one place in the Church. Therefore, as a rule, each church should have only one tabernacle, and this tabernacle must be safe and inviolable.[167]

The place in a church or oratory where the Blessed Sacrament is reserved in the tabernacle should be truly prominent. It ought to be suitable for private prayer so that the faithful may easily and fruitfully, by private devotion also, continue to honor Our Lord in this sacrament. It is therefore, recommended that, as far as

such as retreat houses, hospitals, asylums, orphanages, sanatoriums, and probably Catholic schools and colleges.

---

163. PCI 3 iun. 1918, e.g., an oratory for seminarians and another for the Sisters in domestic charge; the young religious at a summer villa with the rest of the community at the main foundation.
164. c. 1265, 2.
165. **Ibid.,** 3.
166. c. 1269, 3; S.C. Sac. 26 maii 1938.
167. Instr. **Eucharisticum mysterium,** 52.

possible, the tabernacle be placed in a chapel distinct from the middle or central part of the church, above all in those churches where marriages and funerals take place frequently, and in places which are much visited for their artistic or historical treasures.[168]

The Blessed Sacrament is to be reserved in a solid, burglar-proof tabernacle in the center of the high altar or of another altar if this is really outstanding and distinguished. Where there is a lawful custom, and in particular cases to be approved by the local Ordinary, the Blessed Sacrament may be reserved in some other place in the church; but it must be a very special place, having nobility about it, and it must be suitably decorated. It is lawful to celebrate Mass facing the people even if on the altar there is a small but adequate tabernacle.[169]

Care should be taken that the presence of the Blessed Sacrament in the tabernacle is indicated to the faithful by a tabernacle veil or some other suitable means prescribed by competent authority. According to the traditional practices, a lamp should burn continually near the tabernacle as a sign of the honor paid to the Lord.[170]

THE EUCHARIST AS A SACRIFICE

IX. Celebrant of the Eucharist

A. Power and Obligation to Celebrate the Eucharist

The Lord's supper is the assembly or gathering of the people of God, with a priest presiding, to celebrate the memorial of the Lord.[171] When the Church assembles to offer the Sacrifice of the Mass according to the renewed form of celebration, it is made manifest that the Mass is the center of the Church's life.[172] Thus, the celebration of the Eucharist expresses in a particular way the public

168. **Ibid.,** 53.
169. **Ibid.,** 54.
170. **Ibid.,** 57.
171. **Missale Romanum, Inst. Gen.,** II, 7.
172. S.C.C.D., **Instr. Tertia "Liturgicae instaurationes" ad Constitutionem de Sacra Liturgia exsequendam,** 5 sept. 1970.

and social nature of the liturgical actions of the Church, which is the sacrament of unity, namely, the holy people united and ordered under the bishops. The Church is most perfectly displayed in its hierarchic structure in that celebration of the Eucharist at which the bishop presides, surrounded by his priests and ministers, with the active participation of the whole People of God.[173]

In the celebration of the Eucharist priests are also deputed to perform a specific function by reason of a special sacrament, namely, Holy Orders. For they too are dispensers of holy things, especially in the Sacrifice of the Mass. They assume in a unique manner the person of Christ. It is fitting that, by reason of the sign, they participate in the Eucharist and exercise the order proper to them, either by celebrating or concelebrating the Mass, not by limiting themselves to communication like the laity.[174]

By reason of the priesthood itself, all priests are bound by obligation to celebrate Mass several times a year; the bishop and the religious superior, however, are to see to it that they celebrate at least on Sundays and other holydays of obligation.[175] This is commonly considered to be a serious duty arising from divine law; the several times, i.e., three or four times a year, is probably of ecclesiastical law, also binding seriously.[176]

173. Instr. **Eucharisticum mysterium,** 42. **Lumen gentium,** 10: "Though they differ from one another in essence and not only in degree, the common priesthood of the faithful and the ministerial or hierarchical priesthood are nonetheless interrelated. Each of them in its own special way is a participation in the one priesthood of Christ. The ministerial priest, by the sacred power he enjoys, molds and rules the priestly people. **Acting in the person of Christ,** he brings about the Eucharistic Sacrifice and offers it to God in the name of all the people. For their part, the faithful join in the offering of the Eucharist by virtue of their royal priesthood."

174. **Ibid.,** 43. It is of faith that only priests have the power by divine institution to offer the Sacrifice of the Mass. c. 802; cf. Trent. Denz.-Schön. 1752; 1771. Cf. **Summa Theol.,** III, q. 82, aa. 1, 3. "Though all the faithful can baptize, the priest alone can complete the building up of the Body in the Eucharistic Sacrifice" (**Lumen gentium,** 17).

175. c. 805; cf. Trent. sess. XXIII, c. 14, de reform.

176. S.C. Conc. nov. 1696: "A priest who without just cause has not celebrated three or four times in the year, sins mortally

In the mystery of the Sacrifice of the Holy Eucharist, which is the chief task which a priest is called upon to perform, the work of our Redemption is constantly renewed. It is, therefore, earnestly recommended that priests celebrate daily. Even if the faithful cannot be present, the Mass is still the act of Christ and the Church, an action in which the priest is always acting for the salvation of the people.[177] Therefore, priests cannot be easily excused from fault who without reasonable cause abstain from daily celebration, since they would seem to depreciate so great a benefit, both for themselves and for the Church at large, and especially if they would cause scandal or wonderment to the faithful. Should there be an insufficiency of priests in a diocese, the bishop could probably command a priest to offer Mass on Sundays and days of precept so that the faithful could satisfy their obligation.

B. *"Celebret"* or *Approval to Celebrate the Eucharist*

1. Letters of recommendation (*litterae commendatitiae seu testimoniales*) refer to the document by which the local Ordinary or the religious superior testifies to the worthiness of the priest who is his subject and requests the rector of the church to admit him to the celebration of Mass (*celebret*: let him celebrate). A priest who is not attached to the church in which he desires to celebrate

and may be punished by the bishop." Some dispute the authenticity of this decree. **Summa Theol.** III, q. 82, a. 10: "Some have said that a priest may lawfully refrain altogether from consecrating, except that he be bound to do so, and to give the sacraments to the people, by reason of his being entrusted with the care of souls. But this is said quite unreasonably, because everyone is bound to use the grace entrusted to him, when opportunity serves, according to II Cor. 6:1: 'We exhort you that you receive not the grace of God in vain.' But the opportunity of offering sacrifice is considered not merely in relation to the faithful of Christ to whom the sacraments must be administered, but chiefly with regard to God to whom the sacrifice of this sacrament is offered by consecrating. Hence it is not lawful for the priest, even though he has not the care of souls, to refrain altogether from celebrating."

---

177. Instr. **Eucharisticum mysterium,** 44.

Mass shall, unless it is certain that he has in the meantime been guilty of some offense which would require that he be excluded from the celebration of Mass, be permitted to celebrate Mass if he presents an authentic and still valid letter of recommendation of his Ordinary, if he is a secular, or his religious superior, if he is a religious, or of the Sacred Congregation for the Oriental Church, if he belongs to an Oriental rite.[178]

2. If he does not have these letters but it is at once evident to the rector that he is worthy, he can be given permission; but if he is unknown to the rector, he can still receive permission once or twice (i.e., a few times), provided that he be attired in clerical garb, that he receive no recompense on any title from the church for the celebration of Mass, and that he set down in a special book his name, office, and diocese. Special rules laid down by the local Ordinary, consistent with the common law, must be observed by all, even by exempt religious except when they celebrate in the churches of their institute.[179] If a visitor's *celebret* is in order, and if he is not proved guilty of an offense, he cannot be refused permission, even by the local Ordinary, or be required to seek approval by the diocesan curia; if he has no *celebret*, he must be allowed the opportunity to celebrate a few times.

C. Dispositions of the Celebrant

1. Soul

The priest must be in the state of grace in order to celebrate Mass lawfully, and if he is conscious of serious sin, he must confess it before offering the Sacrifice.[180] He should also be without irregularities and censures.

---

178. c. 804, 1.
179. **Ibid.,** 2-3; S.C. Conc. 1 iul. 1926; 18 iul, 1931.
180. c. 807. St. Alphonsus holds that he commits a fourfold sacrilege: 1) consecrating unworthily, 2) receiving unworthily, 3) administering unworthily, 4) administering to the unworthy, viz., himself. Others hold that there are two sins, consecrating and receiving in sin; others that there is one sin (although more grave), since all the acts are ordered to the one Sacrifice.

A priest ought not to fail to prepare himself for the offering of the Eucharistic Sacrifice by devout prayers and after the Sacrifice to give thanks to God for so great a blessing.[181] The remote preparation is the state of grace and a purity of soul which strives to avoid slight sins and the voluntary imperfections which retard the fervor of charity. The proximate preparation consists in the exercise of devotion which dispose the soul for a reverent and fruitful offering of the Sacrifice. To omit all preparation without due cause is slightly sinful; likewise to omit, without reasonable cause, a thanksgiving after Mass, which is due out of reverence for the Real Presence.

The effectiveness of liturgical actions does not consist in the continual search for newer rites or simpler forms, but in an ever deeper insight into the word of God and the mystery which is celebrated. The priest will assure the presence of God and his mystery in the celebration by following the rites of the Church rather than his own preferences. The priest should keep in mind that, by imposing his own personal restoration of sacred rites, he is offending the rights of the faithful and is introducing individualism and idiosyncrasy into celebrations which belong to the whole Church.

The ministry of the priest is the ministry of the Church, and it can be exercised only in obedience, in hierarchical fellowship, and in devotion to the service of God and of his brothers. The hierarchical structure of the liturgy, its sacramental value, and the respect due to the community of the faithful require that the priest exercise his liturgical service as a faithful minister and steward of the mysteries of God. He should not add any rite which is not contained in the liturgical books.[182]

181. c. 810.
182. S.C.C.D., **Instr. Tertia,** 1. **Ibid.:** "Liturgical reform is not at all synonymous with so-called desacralization and is not intended as an occasion for what is called secularization. Thus the liturgy must keep a dignified and sacred character." **Ibid.,** 3: "The liturgical texts composed by the Church also deserve great respect. No one may make changes, substitutions, additions, or deletions in them." Instr. **Eucharisticum mysterium,** 45: "In the celebration of the Eucharist above all, no one, not even a priest, may on his own authority add, omit, or change anything in the liturgy. Only the supreme

2. *Body*

The priest must be free from every defect of body which impedes the celebration of Mass, e.g., blindness, loss of arm or leg,[183] etc. In many cases an Apostolic indult may be obtained.

Priests celebrating the Eucharist must abstain for one hour from solid foods and alcoholic liquids (water is not included), which period of time is to be estimated as one hour before the actual reception of Communion by the celebrant.[184] All priests who are going to celebrate the Eucharist twice or more times may in the prior celebrations take two ablutions as noted in the rubrics of the Missal, but using only water. But if a priest who must celebrate a Mass a second or more times inadvertently takes wine also, in the ablution, he is not prohibited from celebrating the subsequent second or more Masses.[185] Moreover, the local Ordinary may permit priests who celebrate two or more Masses to take something by way of drink even though an interval of one hour does not intervene before the celebration of the next Mass,[186] which permission probably excludes alcoholic drink. This permission may be used even before the first of the series of Masses.

authority of the Church and, according to the provisions of law, the bishop and episcopal conferences, may do this. Priests should therefore ensure that they so preside over the celebration of the Eucharist that the faithful know that they are attending not a rite established on private initiative, but the Church's worship, the regulation of which was entrusted by Christ to the Apostles and their successors." S.C.C.D., 15 maii 1969: "In our day and age there are those who think that they are up-to-date only when they can show off novelty, often bizarre, or devise arbitrary forms of liturgical celebrations. Priests, religious and diocesan, considerate of the true welfare of the faithful, realize that only in a generous and unyielding fidelity to the will of the Church, expressed in its directives, norms, and structures, lies the secret of a lasting and sanctifying pastoral success."

183. Cf. c. 984, 2.
184. Cf. note 88 above.
185. **Christus Dominus,** 7-9.
186. Motu proprio **Pastorale manus,** I, 2.

D. *Minister to Assist the Celebrant*

A priest who celebrates the Eucharist without the presence of a congregation should have a minister to assist him and to make the responses. The latter takes the people's part when suitable. This form of Mass should not be celebrated without a minister except in serious necessity. In this case the greetings and the blessing at the end of Mass are omitted.[187]

In the absence of valid privilege or Apostolic indult, granted personally or for a diocese through the Ordinary, to celebrate the Eucharist, at least habitually, without a minister, in the absence of a congregation, is a serious violation. The traditional liturgical norms of the Church prohibit women (single, married, religious) from serving the priest at the altar, even in chapels of women's homes, convents, schools, and institutes.[188]

X. Conditions for the Celebration of the Eucharist

A. *Place of Celebration*

For the celebration of the Eucharist the people of God is normally assembled in a church, or, if there is none, in some other place worthy of this great mystery. Churches and other places should be suitable for celebrating the Eucharist and for active participation by the faithful.[189] The Ordinary, within his own jurisdiction, will decide when there is a real necessity which permits celebration

---

187. **Missale Romanum, Inst. Gen.,** IV, nn. 209-211. ency. **Mediator Dei:** "On account of the dignity of such an august mystery, it is Our earnest desire, as Mother Church has always commanded, that no priest should say Mass unless a server is at hand to answer the prayers, as canon 813 prescribes."

188. S.C.C.D., **Instr. Tertia,** 7. S.C. Sac. Instr., 1 oct. 1949. This Congregation will grant a Bishop the faculty to permit his priests to say Mass without a server or anyone attending because of the impossibility of finding a server or so that the faithful may attend weekday Mass.

189. **Missale Romanum, Inst. Gen.,** V, n. 253. Cf. S.C.C.D. **Instr. on Masses for special gatherings,** 15 maii 1969.

outside the church. In such a case, careful attention should be given to the choice of a place and a table which are fitting for the Eucharistic Sacrifice. As far as possible, dining halls and tables on which meals are eaten should not be used for the celebration.[190]

The local Ordinary may allow a priest to celebrate Mass on an altar stone outside a sacred place provided the place is respectable and becoming and provided always that it is not a bedroom. The faculty can be granted in individual cases for a just cause but habitually only for a more serious cause.[191] He may also permit priests who possess an indult for a portable altar to use, for a just and serious cause and in place of an altar stone, a Greek antimensium or a linen cloth by the bishop. In the right corner of the cloth must be placed relics of martyrs which have been authenticated by the bishop. Moreover, the other rubrical requirements, especially those concerning altar cloths and corporal, must be observed.[192] These faculties are interpreted in the light of the subsequent norm

190. S.C.C.D., **Instr. Tertia,** 9.
191. Motu proprio **Pastorale munus,** 7. A similar faculty is obtainable by religious in their own religious houses from the competent major superior (Sec. Status, rescript. **Cum admotae,** 6 nov. 1964, n. 4). Cf. c. 822, 4. A purely personal privilege of a portable altar of itself and without explicit mention does not provide the means of fulfilling one's Mass precept, except for the celebrant and the server. Attendance at this Mass in the open (**sub dio**) does satisfy (C. 1249). S.C. Sac., 1 oct. 1949: "The place where a portable altar is set up must be appropriate and decent, or fitting and honorable, lest because of its unworthy and unbecoming character grave injury and irreverence redound to the divine Mysteries. An appropriate place demands security and space, so that the Mass can be offered safely and conveniently without any danger of profanation or of spilling of the Precious Blood from the chalice; a decent place refers to the quality of the place, that is, it demands that the Mass be not celebrated in a bedroom where someone usually sleeps, nor in any other place unbefitting the dignity of so great a Sacrifice. Decency also concerns the immediate place, that is, the table on which the portable altar is laid, that it be not unclean nor devoted to profane uses. This table must be of sufficient length and breadth to afford safe control of the stone, support for the Missal, and a proper and becoming celebration of the Mass."
192. **Ibid.,** 9; cf. **Cum admotae, loc. cit.**

whereby it is not necessary to have a consecrated stone in a movable altar or in the table where the Eucharist is celebrated outside a sacred place.[193] Out of respect for the celebration of the Lord's memorial and the meal in which the Body and Blood of the Lord are eaten, there should be at least one cloth on the altar.[194]

Permission to celebrate the Eucharist for special gatherings, outside a sacred place, can be given only by the local Ordinary; the norms governing such celebrations are to be observed.[195] In cases of celebrations in private houses or institutes the bishop will give permission only if the group gathers where there is no chapel or oratory and only if this is a fitting place for such a celebration. Celebrations in bedrooms are always excluded.[196] Such gatherings are:

a) Gatherings for retreat, religious or pastoral studies, for one or more days, or for meetings of the lay apostolate or similar associations.

b) Meetings for pastoral motives in certain sections of the parish (e.g., so-called home Masses).

c) Gatherings of the faithful who live far from the parish church and who periodically come together to enrich their religious formation.

d) Gatherings of young people or of persons of the same condition or formation, who periodically meet for religious formation or instruction adapted to their mentality.

e) Family gatherings around the sick or aged who cannot leave their house and who otherwise would never participate in the Eucharistic celebration (included are friends and those who look after the sick).

f) Those gathered together for a wake or for some exceptional religious occasion.[197]

For these celebrations outside of a sacred place, especially in

---

193. **Missale Romanum, Inst. Gen.,** V, n. 265.
194. **Ibid.,** n. 268.
195. S.C.C.D., **Instr. on Masses for Special Gatherings,** 15 maii, 1969.
196. **Ibid.,** 4.
197. **Ibid.,** 2.

private houses, Communion under both kinds is excluded; likewise giving Communion to oneself and receiving it in the hand.[198] Moreover:

a) Permission for such Masses may not be given for Sundays and holydays of obligation.

b) The necessity of obtaining the local Ordinary's permission being kept in mind, the pastor should be notified, if the celebrant is not the pastor, and both give a report of the celebrations to the bishop.

c) The norms for the Eucharistic fast should be observed; in no way can the Eucharist be preceded by an agape. If one should follow, it must not be on the same table on which the Eucharist is celebrated.

d) Bread for the Eucharist remains unleavened bread, the only kind permitted in the Latin Church and not without grave reasons. It is to be confected in the customary form.

e) The celebration should not occur late at night.

f) Even in gatherings with family ties no one is to be excluded who desires to participate.[199]

The local Ordinary may permit the celebration of Mass for a just cause at sea and on rivers, provided due safeguards are used.[200] It is probable that Mass may be celebrated in one's stateroom or cabin, provided that there is nothing unbefitting or irreverent present.

Infirm or elderly priests may be permitted by the local Ordinary to celebrate Mass, even on the more solemn feasts, at home but not in a bedroom. The liturgical laws must be observed. Permission to sit can be granted if they are unable to stand.[201]

B. *Time of Celebration*

The beginning of Mass shall not take place earlier than one hour before dawn or later than one hour after noon.[202] All Regulars

---

198. **Ibid.,** 7.
199. **Ibid.,** 10.
200. Motu proprio **Pastorale munus,** 8.
201. **Ibid.,** 10; cf. **Cum admotae,** 5.
202. c. 821, 1.

may in virtue of privilege begin Mass anywhere two hours before dawn and two (and even three) hours after noon; in their own churches also they may, for a just cause, begin Mass two hours after midnight. Visiting priests may be permitted to celebrate Mass in the churches of these Regulars two hours after midnight and two (or three) hours after midday. The local Ordinary (and in religious houses the competent religious superior) may permit priests, for a just cause, to celebrate Mass at any hour of the day and to distribute Communion in the evening, with due observance of the other requirements of law. The special norms for Holy Thursday, Good Friday, and the Easter Vigil, as they are applied in each diocese, should be consulted. On Christmas night only the conventual or the parochial Mass can be commenced at midnight, and no other without an Apostolic indult. But in all religious houses and pious homes, if they have an oratory with the right of habitual reservation of the Blessed Eucharist, on Christmas night one priest can celebrate three Masses of the liturgy or, observing the usual regulations, a single Mass, at which all present may satisfy their obligation of hearing Mass and at which the priest may distribute Holy Communion to those who request it.[203]

C. *Calendar*

On solemnities the celebrant is bound to follow the calendar of the church where he is celebrating, i.e., the diocesan calendar or the calendar proper to the church or oratory where he is celebrating. On Sundays, weekdays of Advent and Lent, feasts and obligatory memorials: a) if Mass is celebrated with a congregation, he should follow the calendar of the church where he is celebrating; b) if Mass is celebrated without a congregation, he may choose the calendar of the church or the calendar he normally follows.

On optional memorials the priest may choose the Mass of the weekday, of the saint of the day, or of one of the saints commemorated or mentioned in the martyrology of that day, a Mass for a

---

203. **Ibid.,** 2-3. The doors may be open and strangers admitted to the Masses (PCI 5 mart. 1954).

various occasion, or a votive Mass. On a weekday of the year he may choose the weekday Mass, the Mass of a saint mentioned in the martyrology that day, a Mass for a various occasion, or a votive Mass.[204]

D. *Bination or Number of Masses*

With the exception of Christmas and All Souls' Day, on which it is allowed to offer the Eucharistic Sacrifice three times, it is not permitted a priest to celebrate Mass more often than once a day, except with an Apostolic indult or with the faculty granted by the local Ordinary. The local Ordinary can permit priests, because of the scarcity of clergy and for a just cause, to celebrate Mass twice on weekdays and even three times on Sundays and holydays of obligation provided that genuine pastoral necessity so demands.[205]

The local Ordinaries of the U.S.A. have the faculty, in accord with their judgment and conscience, to permit priests to celebrate Mass three times on Saturdays and days preceding holydays of obligation, provided the first and second Masses are celebrated for weddings and funerals and the third Mass is celebrated in the evening so that the precept may be satisfied by the faithful. The acceptance of a stipend is prohibited, except for a single Mass.[206]

Bination is not a privilege of convenience or a personal privilege, but it is granted for the benefit of the faithful. The prudent judgment of the necessity (which is made by the local Ordinary but called to his attention by the pastors) is to be based upon a wide interpretation, i.e., it is sufficient that a notable number of the faithful will otherwise not attend Mass. It is also necessary that no priest is *able* and *willing* to say Mass at the hour convenient for the people. A local Ordinary could require one of his own priests to celebrate in order to avoid bination, but not force a visiting priest to do so, even if the latter were saying a Mass in another place in the parish or even in the same church but at

---

204. **Missale Romanum, Inst. Gen.**, VII, nn. 314-316.
205. Motu proprio **Pastorale munus,** 2.
206. S.C. Sac. 20 ian. 1970.

an hour inconvenient for the people. In charity and courtesy a visiting priest will be prepared to help in the needs of the place, but he is not strictly obliged; the pastor is also to accommodate his request, as far as possible, to the convenience of the visitor. The pastor is not obliged at great inconvenience to make this request of another priest. A pastor may not indiscriminately add to his list of Masses or change his schedules if this will require bination which is not based on the cause noted in the law. Permission of the local Ordinary to binate can be presumed in an unexpected situation, e.g., illness of the scheduled celebrant. Any priest who supplies for one who has the faculty to binate may also say a second Mass. The number of faithful who would be deprived of Mass unless a priest binated is commonly judged to be between ten and thirty, but in the variability of actual circumstances the Church leaves it up to the prudent judgment of the local Ordinary and the one who binates, e.g., the need for Viaticum, the need of a community, hospital, school, etc. which would otherwise be without Mass.

E. Concelebration

Concelebration of the Eucharist aptly demonstrates the unity of the Sacrifice and of the priesthood. Moreover, whenever the faithful take an active part, the unity of the People of God is strikingly manifested, particularly if the bishop presides. Concelebration both symbolizes and strengthens the brotherly bond of the priesthood, because by virtue of the sacred ordination and mission which they have in common, all priests are bound together in close brotherhood.

Therefore, unless it conflicts with the needs of the faithful, which must always be consulted with the deepest pastoral concern, and although every priest retains the right to celebrate alone, it is desirable that priests should celebrate the Eucharist in this eminent manner. This applies both to communities of priests and to groups which gather on particular occasions, as also to all similar circumstances. Those who live in community or serve the same church should welcome visiting priests into their concelebration. The competent superiors should therefore facilitate and indeed positively encourage concelebration, whenever pastoral needs or other reasonable motives do not prevent it.[207]

It is the local Ordinary who gives the general guidelines or disciplinary regulations governing concelebration in the diocese, even in churches and semi-public oratories of exempt religious communities. Every Ordinary, including the major superior of non-exempt clerical religious institutes and of societies of clerics living in community without vows, has the right to judge the suitability of, and to give permission for, concelebration in his churches and oratories[208] without the need to consult the local Ordinary. He may also limit the number of concelebrants.

Where there is a large number of priests, the competent superior may permit concelebration several times on the same day, but at different times or in distinct places.[209] No one may concelebrate in a Mass which has already begun.[210]

Without further permission concelebration is permitted at: 1) the chrism Mass and the evening Mass on Holy Thursday; 2) councils, meetings of bishops, and synods; 3) the blessing of an abbot. With permission of the Ordinary: 1) at the conventual Mass and at the principal Mass in churches and oratories when the need of the faithful does not require that all the priests present celebrate individually; 2) at any kind of meeting of priests, either secular or regular: at Masses celebrated on the occasion of a synod or pastoral visitation or whenever priests meet their bishop during a retreat or any other gathering.[211]

In addition to any other faculty to binate or trinate, without further permission it is permissible to celebrate or concelebrate more than once on the same day in the following cases: 1) one who has celebrated or concelebrated the chrism Mass on Holy Thursday may also celebrate or concelebrate the evening Mass; 2) one who has celebrated the Easter Vigil Mass may celebrate or concelebrate

207. Instr. **Eucharisticum mysterium,** 47.
208. **Missale Romanum, Inst. Gen.,** n. 155.
209. **Ibid.,** n. 154.
210. **Ibid.,** n. 156.
211. **Ibid.,** nn. 153, 157.

the second Mass at Easter; 3) all priests may concelebrate the three Masses at Christmas, provided these are celebrated at the proper times; 4) one who concelebrates with the bishop or his delegate at a synod, at a pastoral visitation, or at a gathering of priests for any reason may celebrate another Mass *for the benefit of the faithful* if the bishop so decides. This holds also for meetings of religious with their own Ordinary.[212]

XI. Application of the Sacrifice of the Mass

A. *Notion*

1. The value of the Mass is the intrinsic power which it enjoys to produce its effects or fruits. In itself the Sacrifice of the Mass has an infinite value and efficacy, since Christ, who is of infinite dignity, is both Priest or principal offerer and the sacrificial Victim. Moreover, being substantially the same sacrifice as that of the Cross, it possesses the same infinite value and sufficiency. Thus any one Mass in itself is capable of truly infinite praise and glorification of God, of thanksgiving and propitiation to him, of securing from him the remission of all sins and punishment whatsoever, as well as beseeching all possible goods and inexhaustible benefits. The Mass, of absolutely infinite value in itself, has a capability which is infinite both intensively and extensively, i.e., as regards the degrees of its effects and as regards the number of its effects and the individuals sharing in them. In other words, it is not possible to assign limits to the efficacy of the Mass either in the number and in the quality of its fruits. It is only in comparison with this essential and proper value and efficacy that the concomitant effectiveness of the impetration, the merit and satisfaction of the Church, of the priest or secondary minister, and of the assisting faithful is to be considered, i.e., inasmuch as the Mass is also man's oblation.

2. Of the effects which are accomplished by the Mass, the goods and benefits attained or ends and purposes achieved, some

212. **Ibid.,** n. 158. Cf. S.C.C.D., declaratio, 7 aug. 1972.

of them, viz., the latreutic or the worship of adoration and the eucharistic or the thanksgiving directly regard God and are infallible and automatic (*ex opere operato*), since due to the holiness and merits of Christ, this Sacrifice is always and unfailingly pleasing and acceptable to God; the others, viz., the impetratory or the entreaties for spiritual and temporal goods, the propitiatory or the reconciliation with God, and the satisfactory or the remission of sins and their temporal punishment, directly regard man and are the fruits and benefits accruing to man from the Mass.[213] These latter especially are called the *fruits of the Mass* and are received in a limited degree and extent. Creatures are not capable of infinite goods. Moreover, the Mass cannot have greater efficacy regarding man than the Sacrifice of the Cross itself, or the sacraments which derive their power from the Cross. Even though the Sacrifice of the Cross is infinite *in itself*, it remains limited *in its application;* otherwise all men would be automatically justified and saved, as likewise one Mass would suffice to save the whole world and eliminate Purgatory. This is the practice of the Church in repeatedly offering Masses to apply both for different persons and also for the same person and for the same benefit. Thus, as with the Sacrifice of the Cross, the Sacrifice of the Mass in the *application* of its effects, in its fruits directed toward man's welfare, depends not only upon the efficacy of the principal cause, Christ, but also upon the dispositions, the willingness or acceptance of those for whom entreaty, propitiation, or satisfaction are offered.[214] These fruits may also

213. Cf. Trent, Denz.-Schön. 1739-1743; 1751-1753.

214. **Summa Theol.**, III, q. 79, aa. 5, 7 ad 2. Pius XII, ency. **Mediator Dei**: "Now the Apostle of the Gentiles proclaims the copious plenitude and perfection of the Sacrifice of the Cross, when he says that Christ by one oblation has perfected forever them that are sanctified. For the merits of this Sacrifice, since they are altogether boundless and immeasurable, know no limits; for they are meant for all men of every time and place. This follows from the very fact that in this Sacrifice the God-Man is the Priest and Victim; that his immolation was entirely perfect, as was his obedience to the will of his Eternal Father; and also that he suffered death as the Head of the human race. . . . This purchase, however, does not immediately have its full effect; since Christ after redeeming

increase as a result of the special prayers of the Church, e.g., in a votive or *requiem Mass*, or because of greater external solemnity, e.g., a sung Mass, or due to additional ways of entering into the offering of the Mass, e.g., by offering an alms or stipend for the application of the Mass and also participation in the very Mass offered.

3. The benefits or fruits received by man from the Mass are threefold:

a. *General Benefits*. These are by their nature ordained to the good of the whole Church, i.e., of all the faithful, living and departed, who place no obstacle, and even of others that they too might enter into full Communion with the Church. As the unbloody repetition of the Sacrifice of the Cross, the Mass is likewise offered up for all; it is essentially an act of public worship. No special application of the celebrant is required beyond a general intention to celebrate according to the mind of the Church. These benefits or fruits are not lessened by the number of individuals sharing in them.

b. *Special or Ministerial Benefits*. These are applied to some person or purpose by intention of the priest. This is the portion of the fruits or benefits of the Mass which is left to the free application or disposal of the celebrant through the intention he formulates. He alone takes the place of Christ and acts in his person in offering the Sacrifice, and thus he alone applies its fruits. The share of

---

the world at the lavish cost of his own Blood, still must come into complete possession of the souls of men. Wherefore, that the redemption and salvation of each person and of future generations unto the end of time may be effectively accomplished and be acceptable to God, it is necessary that men should individually come into vital contact with the Sacrifice of the Cross, so that the merits which flow from it might be imparted to them. . . . The cooperation of the faithful is required so that sinners may be individually purified in the Blood of the Lamb. For though, speaking generally, Christ reconciled by his painful death the whole human race with the Father, he wishes that all should approach and be drawn to the Cross, especially by means of the sacraments and the Eucharistic Sacrifice, to obtain the salutary fruits produced by him upon it."

each one in these benefits is probably diminished as they are applied to more persons or purposes.

c. *Most Special Benefits.* This is the portion of the benefits or fruits which is proper to the priest who offers the Mass and which always accrues to himself; likewise, very special fruits are received by those who in some particular way are united with the priest in offering the Sacrifice, e.g., servers, assistants, attendants at Mass, offerers of the bread and wine, etc. The more intimately one shares in the offering of the Mass, the more fully its benefits are enjoyed. It is improbable that the priest can apply his very special fruits to another, and it is unlawful when the Mass is applied in justice.[215] The number of persons enjoying these benefits does not lessen them.

4. The application of the Mass, therefore, is the particular determination or disposition which the celebrant makes of the benefits to be enjoyed from the Holy Sacrifice. The beneficiary derives special impetratory, propitiatory, and satisfactory effects, while at the same time adoration and thanksgiving are offered in his name. It is certain teaching that the priest alone has this power by his intention to apply the benefits or fruits of the Mass.[216]

B. *Intention*

1. The intention of applying the Mass must be made by the celebrant. It is commonly taught that for validity this intention must be *at least habitual* and *implicit, absolute* or equivalently such. The intention once made must not be retracted, since the application is made in the manner of a donation or transferral of the benefits or fruits, and thus remains valid until revoked. The intention must be made *at least before the consecration,*[217] since

---

215. Alexander VII, 24 sept. 1665, prop. 8 condemned (Denz.-Schön, 2028): "A priest can lawfully accept a twofold stipend for the same Mass by applying to the petitioner even the most special part of the fruits appropriated to the celebrant himself, and this after the decree of Urban VIII."
216. Pius VI, 28 aug. 1794 (Denz.-Schön. 2630).
217. It is probable that the intention may be made after the con-

the essence of the Sacrifice is in the consecration of both species. An actual and explicit intention is always preferrable; in practice a priest should always formulate his intention before beginning Mass (although he may do so some time in advance), so that all the prayers of the Mass might benefit the person or purpose for which the Mass is to be applied. The intention once made must not be retracted before the consecration is completed, if it is to retain its validity and effectiveness.

2. The intention must be absolute and cannot be conditioned on a future event, since the intention is thereby suspended and the Mass is not offered for that intention. Thus, a Mass cannot be said under the condition that someone will later request a Mass (a stipend cannot be accepted for this),[218] nor for a person under the condition that they will leave the celebrant a legacy, nor for a living person that it will benefit his soul after his death. Equivalently absolute is a condition of the present or past, e.g., if John is not already dead; if I have not already satisfied this stipend, I intend to do so now; if I have, I intend to apply this Mass for such-and-such a person or purpose; if this purpose is not realizable now, I intend this other purpose; etc.

3. The celebrant's intention must be *sufficiently determined at least implicitly, to a certain person or purpose*. It suffices that he conform his will to the intention explicitly formulated by another, e.g., the intention of the giver,[219] the one noted in the Mass book, the intention of the superior or the sacristan (assuming that it exists), according to the order of stipends received, etc.; the intention is thus objectively and exactly determined and it is not

secration of the bread and before that of the wine. However, in practice, at least for a Mass to be applied under any title of obligation, the priest should in such a case apply another Mass for the intention.

---

218. c. 825, 1º. If a priest, hearing that a person has died, knows for certain that someone will shortly request a Mass for the deceased, his application of the Mass will be valid. But after receiving the stipend he is freed from the obligation of applying another Mass only if the donor of the stipend knows what has been done and agrees to it.

219. Cf. S.C. Conc. 27 feb. 1915; S. Poen. 7 dec. 1892.

necessary that the person or purpose be known or explicitly determined by the priest. It is permitted to apply a number of Masses to a number of persons or purposes collectively when the priest is unable to remember or does not know the precise order of precedence in the obligations undertaken (whether from the same or from several donors), e.g., ten Masses for the ten obligations undertaken; thus one-tenth share in each Mass is gained by each of the ten and the whole benefit enjoyed upon completion of the ten Masses. It is an invalid intention which is directed to some one on a list without further determination of which one. If the celebrant makes a simple error in application, thinking that the Mass was for a deceased man instead of a woman or a living rather than a deceased person, the application is valid, since normally his intention to fulfill his duty is considered to center on the person for whom applied and not the circumstance.

4. If the priest has made several different intentions for the same Mass and he has no prevailing or overriding intention for such situations, it is commonly considered that the last intention formulated is the one that is satisfied, being the more actual and the stronger expression of his will. If he has a predominant will in this matter or prevailing intention, then that one is satisfied, e.g., if his prevailing intention is always to say the Mass for which there is the greater obligation, such as a Gregorian series Mass over a manual Mass or a special date obligation over one without attached circumstance. If both intentions made are equal, e.g., two different Gregorian Masses for the same day, it is considered that the second or last made intention is fulfilled. In any doubt, a second Mass can be celebrated on another day for the intention that was not said. If the priest makes no intention or application in the Mass, or one which is invalid, the special or ministerial benefits or fruits probably redound to himself (especially if he has made such a general intention—or to anyone else whom he has intended), or go into the spiritual treasury of the Church. It is recommended that a priest formulate sound prevailing intentions and renew them from time to time.

5. A second intention in the Mass is the will that the Mass benefit another person or purpose, inasmuch as it does not prejudice

the primary intention or application. This is always lawful. It also provides an alternative application of the benefits or fruits in the event that the primary intention for some reason is inapplicable. At the intercessions for the living and of the dead in the Eucharist Prayer (according to the text selected) as many persons or purposes as desired may be included, as these remembrances are not really applications of the Mass but a form of impetration deriving its special value from association with the Holy Sacrifice. Moreover, the special or ministerial fruits of the Mass may be divided and applied variously, e.g., the impetratory for one, the propitiatory for another, the satisfactory for the departed, etc., even the same fruits being applied to both living and dead. However, this may be done only in those Masses which are not celebrated under any title of obligation in justice, since in the latter case it is considered that the whole benefit of the Mass is willed by the one to whom it is due.

C. For Whom Application May Be Made

1. The Mass may be applied to all the *living* without distinction, as long as the Church places no restrictions.[220] Mass may be offered privately for those who are excommunicated and also for a *vitandus* but only for his conversion.[221] Baptized non-Catholics and even the unbaptized may have Mass said for them (the priest even accepting a stipend), but not publicly and no scandal must be given by this celebration.[222] By private celebration is meant the Mass is not announced and that only the priest or a few know for whom it is being applied, e.g., the family or a few friends. Even if the celebration is public, the application must be secret and always scandal must be avoided. Mass may not be applied publicly for those who have been denied Christian burial.[223] Mass may be publicly said for rulers of the state for the good government and prosperity of the State; likewise upon their death. Mass may be

---

220. Cf. c. 809; Trent. Denz.-Schön. 1743; 1753.
221. c. 2262, 2, 2o.
222. S. Off. 12 iul. 1865.
223. c. 1241.

said for the saints in heaven and for the angels, but only to implore
an increase in the worship and external honor of them among men,
or to beseech God for spiritual or temporal favors through their
merits and intercession, or to thank him for the benefits received
through them.

2. Mass may also be applied for all the dead who are in
Purgatory.[224] Mass is certainly profitable for the suffering souls
in Purgatory, but it is not certain to what extent it profits them or
whether a certain soul alone profits. Consequently, it is the practice
of the Church to celebrate many Masses for the dead and to pray
for all the dead in each Mass. Application of the Mass for the
damned in hell is invalid; likewise, for infants who are in limbo.
Mass may not be applied for baptized infants who die before reaching
the use of reason; the Mass of the day or, the rubrics permitting,
a votive Mass of the Angels may be celebrated for the intention of
the donor, for the family in thanksgiving for the benefits received
by the infant of the family, etc. Unless specified in a diocesan regulation, the stipend for such a Mass is not equivalent to that for
the exequies of an adult. Those heretics, schismatics, the excommunicated and sinners who gave signs of repentance before death
and who can be given Christian burial may have Mass said for
them publicly, otherwise privately.[225] For the deceased unbaptized
Mass may be applied privately and even publicly, if, as in the case
of catechumens, they gave signs of conversion and can be given
Christian burial.[226] For those who have been denied Christian burial
no funeral for anniversary Mass nor any public Mass may be celebrated.[227] A Requiem Mass is of more benefit to the departed, not
substantially but sometimes accidentally, because of the special
prayers recited.[228]

---

224. Cf. note 220 above. **Summa Theol., Suppl.,** q. 71, a. 2, ad 3.
225. Cf. c. 1240.
226. Cf. c. 1239.
227. c. 1241.
228. **Summa Theol. Suppl.,** q. 71, a. 9, ad. 5: "In the office of the
     Mass there is not only a sacrifice but also prayers. . . . As
     regards the sacrifice offered the Mass profits equally the de-
     parted, no matter in whose honor it be said: and this is the
     principal thing done in the Mass. But as regards the prayers,

XII. Obligation of Applying the Mass

A. *Promise*

A promise is a deliberate and spontaneous obligation of faith to another to do or to omit some thing or action. It obliges only after its acceptance and from the virtue of fidelity. A promise obliges in justice only when the one promising so intends to bind himself and it is so understood by the one accepting it. One can also vow to say a Mass and thus the obligation will bind gravely or lightly by the virtue of religion according as the one making the vow intends.

A free or gratuitous promise given to apply a Mass obliges from fidelity and only lightly, since there is no intention of seriously binding oneself, unless such is expressly intended and accepted. The promise is usually given more for the purpose of showing good will rather than of binding oneself seriously. There must be a true and serious promise (although not a serious obligation) which has been so accepted by another, otherwise it may be the expression merely of a resolve, or may be made casually or without any purpose of binding oneself, etc., and thus its fulfillment does not bind under sin. One who intends to bind himself seriously and it is so accepted, or who undertakes a quasi contract, e.g., a priest who has accepted many benefits and who has promised the benefactor a Mass in gratitude and remuneration, is bound seriously and in justice to fulfill the *onerous* promise made; likewise if one has promised to undertake to fulfill the obligation of another. Unless it is an onerous promise that has been made, several promises may be satisfied by the same single Mass, e.g., a promise made to one person to say a Mass for his deceased relative, to another for his intention. The promise made by members of a pious confra-

---

that Mass is most profitable in which the prayers are appointed for this purpose. Nevertheless, this defect may be supplied by the greater devotion either of the one who says the Mass or of the one who orders the Mass to be said, or again by the intercession of the saint whose suffrage is besought in the Mass."

ternity or association to say a Mass or Masses for deceased members, etc., is an onerous obligation. Unless it is expressly understood to be such, it is not certain that such an obligation binds in strict justice or that one sins seriously in failing to fulfill it.

B. *Pious Foundation*

Stipends derived from the income of foundations are called funded, or funded Masses,[229] since the duty to celebrate and apply the Masses is founded upon an endowment. A foundation for Masses, as any other foundation, is an endowment or capital established perpetually or for a long time and entrusted, with written permission of the local Ordinary,[230] or the religious Ordinary in the case of exempt religious,[231] to an ecclesiastical moral person for the purpose of celebrating Masses from the income derived from it for the period of the foundation; this obligation to which the moral person is bound, after legitimate acceptance, is in virtue of an innominate, synallagmatic or reciprocal contract: *"do ut facias."*[232] There must be an acceptance by the moral person, the permission of the competent authority, and the investment of the endowment.[233] The recipient of an income from a foundation is called the beneficiary or chaplain. Unless the founder has established the stipend, the obligations of the foundation must be reckoned by the diocesan custom or tax for funded Masses or by the stipend set by the religious Ordinary in the case of exempt religious.[234]

A beneficiary is obliged in strict justice to celebrate and to apply funded Masses, since this is in the manner of a bilateral contract. The obligation is serious not only as to the number to be said but also as to whatever circumstances are attached, e.g., place, time, quality of Mass, etc. The reduction of burdens attached to a pious foundation is reserved exclusively to the Apostolic See, unless a contrary provision is contained in the articles of foundation; the

229. cc. 826, 3; 1544.
230. c. 1546.
231. c. 1550.
232. c. 1544.
233. Cf. cc. 1547; 1550.
234. Cf. cc. 1545; 1550.

local Ordinary in particular circumstances may make certain reductions.[235]

C. *Obedience*

The bishop and the religious superior are to take care to see that their subjects celebrate at least on Sundays and other days of precept.[236] Ecclesiastical superiors can command the priests who are subject to them to celebrate and even to apply Mass, as this is connected with the external ministry and public worship. Examples of this are seen in the obligation of the Mass *pro populo* and the third Mass on All Souls' Day for the intention of the Holy Father. A secular or religious priest who applies Mass for other than the intention commanded by his superior validly applies the Mass but unlawfully.

The religious superior can command his subject to apply a Mass for a stipend which the superior has accepted and the obligation thus contracted by the superior is transferred to the subject. The subject is then bound seriously in justice and in obedience to satisfy the Mass. The superior may prescribe that a subject say a Mass in obedience and for which no stipend is involved, e.g., a Mass of thanksgiving, for some community favor, for benefactors, etc. The subject is bound in obedience either seriously or slightly according as the superior has imposed the obligation. A subject is also often bound by his Constitutions to celebrate a certain number of Masses and for special intentions; he is bound in such instances in the manner in which his laws bind in his Institute, usually not under sin.[237] A confessor in the internal forum may command the application of Mass as a sacramental penance.

The religious superior should not in prudence question the occasional omission or the one or another failure of a subject to

235. Cf. E 11 below.
236. c. 805.
237. S.C. Rel. 3 maii 1914: "Q. Can religious superiors command their subjects also in virtue of holy obedience to celebrate according to the intention prescribed by the Constitutions or established by these superiors, saving the exceptions sanctioned by the Constitutions or by legitimate custom? R. In the affirmative."

celebrate daily Mass, when this seems attributable to valid and good reasons and, when given the manner of living and attitude of the particular subject, an explanation does not appear to be warranted. However, the superior should question when his precept or order has been neglected or violated, or a Mass for some public reason, e.g., parish Mass, Sisters' community Mass, etc., is omitted or the omission might cause scandal, e.g., when it is frequent or over some days, or when the general order and discipline of the community is being affected or the discharge of stipend and other obligations is impaired.

D. *Pastorate*

1. *Obligation*

"Since by divine precept it is enjoined on all to whom is entrusted the care of souls to know their sheep, to offer sacrifice for them,"[238] a pastor[239] by a sort of contract whereby he is supported by his flock is bound *in justice* to procure and promote the spiritual welfare of those entrusted to his care, which is more efficaciously accomplished by applying the fruits of the Mass for them. Thus, based fundamentally on divine law and immediately on ecclesiastical law, a pastor is certainly bound to celebrate and apply Mass for the people (*Missa pro populo*) on certain stated days in the year. Religious superiors as such, although they are pastors over their communities and by divine law are bound to offer Mass sometimes for their subjects, are not bound by the particular dispositions of canon law for the *Missa pro populo*. A vicar econome or administrator of a parish,[240] a quasi pastor[241] and a pastor in a mission diocese[242] are also bound by this obligation. No other parochial vicars or chaplains as such are subject to this law.[242a]

238. Trent. sess. XXIII, c. 1 **de reform;** Heb. 5:1.
239. c. 451, 1.
240. c. 473, 1; probably also the senior curate or nearest pastor who by c. 472,2⁰ assumes interim administration of the parish, but only for this period.
241. c. 466.
242. S.C.P.F. 16 maii 1933; 26 ian. 1954.
242a. Military chaplains are subject to special norms.

2. Requisites

Pastors in virtue of their pastoral office are bound to apply Mass for the people on the days prescribed by the Church.[243] A low Mass suffices. If one of the feasts falls on a Sunday, only one Mass is applied; likewise only one is applied on Christmas Day.[244] The obligation, binding in strict justice, is both personal and real, i.e., attached to the office. It must be satisfied in person by the pastor, or if he is legitimately impeded, by another on the prescribed day; if a justifying cause prevents the offering of the Mass on the proper day even through another, he must offer it as soon as possible.[245] It is said only for the living members of the congregation. The nature of the serious obligation is such that it always remains intact, i.e., it is not removed by any excusing cause. There is a light obligation to say the Mass in person, at the prescribed time or place, but the sin is serious if the last two are habitually violated. A pastor, and also a vicar econome, in charge of two parishes *aeque principaliter* united, offers only one Mass.[246] No stipend may be taken for the *Missa pro populo*, nor for the second Mass in the case of bination.[247]

A pastor's failure to celebrate Mass for the people on the prescribed day is without fault when there is a good reason, such as illness, an irregularity, legitimate absence from the parish, the obligation to say a conventual Mass, etc. When the pastor is faced with saying another Mass on one of the prescribed days, e.g., a Requiem or nuptial Mass, he should seek permission of the local Ordinary to transfer the Mass for the people to another day, which permission the Ordinary may grant,[248] and which in many dioceses is generally granted to pastors. The place for offering the Mass is the parish church, unless circumstances require or advise its celebration elsewhere; a pastor lawfully absent from his parish may offer this Mass in the place where he is or through the priest taking

243. Cf. cc. 466, 1; 339, 1.
244. C. 339, 2.
245. **Ibid.,** 4; 466, 3.
246. c. 466, 2; PCI 14 iul, 1922.
247. c. 824, 2.
248. c. 466, 3.

his place in the parish.[249] Provided that the Mass is offered on the prescribed day, a less weighty reason justifies its being offered elsewhere than in the parish church or through another there. The local Ordinary need not be approached.

3. *Prescribed Days*

At the present time the *Missa pro populo* obliges on the days contained in the following taxative list: all Sundays and days of precept which oblige in the place where the care of souls is located.[250]

E. *Stipend or Alms*

1. *Notion*

A stipend is a sum of money or some other thing of value which is given to a priest for his maintenance with the understanding that he will offer the Sacrifice of the Mass for a determined purpose.[251] The obligation is one of commutative justice arising from an onerous innominate contract *"do ut facias"* by which the priest is bound in justice to say the Mass or to restore the stipend if he does not or will not celebrate, and the person who has promised a stipend is bound in justice to give it when the Mass has been celebrated. The priest's obligation to satisfy the stipend is certainly serious, regardless of the smallness or largeness of the stipend, since the privation of the special or ministerial fruits is a notable damage.

2. *Lawfulness*

According to the traditional and approved usage of the Church it is permitted to every priest celebrating and applying a Mass to accept a stipend.[252] The Mass is one source of support for the priest, who serving at the altar may live by the altar,[253] even those

---

249. **Ibid.,** 4-5.
250. S.C. pro clero, **Decretum,** 25 iul, 1970.
251. Some consider that "stipend" comes from **stips** or a small contribution in money, and **pendere** or to weigh: thus originally a soldier's pay.
252. c. 824, 1.
253. Cf. I Cor. 9:7, 13-14; **Summa Theol.,** II-II, q. 100, a. 2. To hold that it is a base abuse to receive alms for the celebration

who are privately wealthy; sustenance refers only to a part of the day. Only if the stipend would be considered as the price of the Mass and as though the priest would not offer the Mass if the stipend were not forthcoming would there be simony.[254]

If a priest celebrates Mass more than once a day and applies one Mass under an obligation of justice, except on Christmas, he cannot take a stipend for another Mass but only some compensation based on a claim extrinsic to the application of the Mass.[255] A serious sin of disobedience would be committed but no restitution of the additional stipend would be required, since the application would be valid and an injustice not committed. Extrinsic claims justifying compensation for celebrating a second Mass would be, e.g., the hour at which the second Mass would be said, the inconvenience or expense of the journey to celebrate the Mass or the loss entailed, the second Mass was sung rather than recited, etc. Sometimes an Apostolic indult permits local and religious Ordinaries to allow the acceptance of a second stipend in a bination, (or third in a trination) but the purpose for which the second (and even third) stipend may be accepted is specified.[256] It is never permitted to receive a stipend for a Mass which must be applied in virtue of another obligation, or to accept two stipends for the application of one Mass, or to take one stipend for the celebration of the Mass and another for the application of the same Mass, unless it is certain that one stipend was given for the celebration without the application,[257] e.g., a person about to make a journey wished to attend Mass on that day at a very early hour and offers a stipend for that to the priest with the understanding that he can apply the Mass at will.

In a bination, when two (or more) Masses are said on the same

of Masses and the administration of the sacraments is condemned as false, temerarious, harmful to ecclesiastical and pastoral rights, and injurious to the Church and her ministers (Pius VI, 28 aug. 1794. Denz.-Schön. 2654).

---

254. Cf. c. 727.
255. c. 824, 2. Three stipends are permitted by law on Christmas alone.
256. The entire stipend must be turned over to the Ordinary, even if it exceeds the diocesan tax (S.C. Conc. 9 maii 1920).
257. c. 825, 2-4. Violation involves a serious obligation of restitution.

day and when one of them is said for a stipend or is *pro populo*, the second or other Mass may be said for an obligation arising from charity, vow, precept of a superior, statute or regulation in a confraternity or clerical union to which the priest belongs.[258] It is more commonly held that an obligation incumbent upon a priest-member of a clerical union or society or other organization does not bind in strict justice and thus the priest can satisfy, e.g., his suffrage for deceased members, by the second Mass.[259] A religious may in this way satisfy his personal obligation of suffrage Masses prescribed by his own Constitutions.

Although a priest may not accept a stipend for a second Mass when he binates, when he has already discharged an obligation in justice in the first Mass, he may, however, apply his second Mass gratuitously or in charity for the intention of a person who offers him a stipend for the application of that Mass, and then discharge the justice obligation of the stipend on a subsequent day. Thus, if a donor cannot be put off to another day for the celebration of the Mass or it is not expedient to do so, the priest may choose thus to apply two Masses for the same intention, the bination Mass out of gratitude or charity and another Mass on a subsequent day as the stipend Mass, all of which more than satisfies his obligation to the donor.

3. *Kinds of Stipends*[260]

Stipends which are offered by the faithful for Masses, whether because of their personal piety, as it were from hand to hand, or because of an obligation, even a perpetual one, imposed by a testator on his heirs are called *manual* stipends.

Similar to manual stipends (*ad instar manualium*) are stipends for funded Masses when these cannot be applied at the place designated or by the persons obligated in the articles of foundation and

---

258. c. 825, 2, forbids the reception of a stipend for a Mass owed under any title, not only in justice but also in obedience, fidelity, etc. Thus there cannot be a twofold application of the primary intention.
259. Cf. S.C. Conc. 14 sept. 1878; 5 mart. 1887.
260. c. 826, 1-3.

thus in accordance with the law or Apostolic indult are to be sent to other priests so that the obligations might be satisfied.

The stipends obtained from the income of foundations are called *funded* stipends or funded Masses.

4. *Amount of the Stipend*

It is the right of the local Ordinary to fix for his diocese the manual stipend for Masses by a decree enacted, if possible, in the diocesan synod; and it is not permitted to a priest to demand a larger one. Where there is no decree of the Ordinary the custom of the diocese is to be observed. Even exempt religious are obliged to abide by the Ordinary's decree or diocesan custom regarding manual stipends.[261] The Mass stipend is not to be considered the sole source of income needed by a priest for his livelihood.

To demand a stipend higher than the diocesan stipend is in itself a serious violation of commutative justice and requires restitution. If it is voluntarily offered, a priest may accept such a higher stipend, as willingness on the part of the donor is sufficient title for the acceptance and the Ordinary may not forbid this.[262] A stipend larger than the determined amount may be requested lawfully only by reason of some extrinsic title or circumstance or special inconvenience, e.g., a sung Mass, Mass at a considerable distance or late hour, etc., but not because of the spiritual considerations or special graces connected with a Mass, such as Mass on a privileged altar or at some shrine of pilgrimage.[263] Preference may be given to larger stipends and this made publicly known. On the other hand, unless the Ordinary has forbidden it, it is permissible for a priest to accept a smaller stipend.[264] Even with such a prohibition, a priest may offer Mass for anyone he chooses without accepting any stipend at all.

5. *Number of Stipends to be Satisfied*

The number of Masses that are to be celebrated and applied are to equal the number of stipends given and accepted, no matter

261. c. 831, 1-3.
262. c. 832; S.C. Conc. 16 ian 1649.
263. Cf. c. 918.
264. c. 832.

how small they may be.[265] Even when the stipend is very small or when it is below the diocesan norm, there is a serious obligation entailed and restitution is involved in its violation.[266] Even though stipends which have already been accepted should be lost without any fault on the part of him who has the obligation of celebrating the Mass, the obligation does not cease.[267]

If anyone shall have contributed a sum of money for the application of Masses without indicating the number, this is to be determined on the basis of the stipend of the place where the donor was staying, unless a contrary intention on his part should be lawfully presumed.[268] The presumption must be at least highly probable, but certainty is not required; on the basis of strong positive indications of the donor's intention in the case (e.g., in a letter, in a legacy, will or bequest) to give a larger stipend, together with indications to the contrary, the balance of the probabilities must weigh in favor of the more liberal intention in order to take a larger stipend. Thus if the donor customarily gave larger stipends, considered the diocesan norm too low, directed the Masses to be said in a poor place where the stipend is extremely low, etc., basis for judgment is present. In interpreting bequests, if nothing has been said about the nature of the Masses to be said, e.g., sung or recited, the mind of the testator is ordinarily to be understood to favor recited Masses according to the ordinary stipend; in peculiar circumstances indicating otherwise, the Holy See should be consulted.[269]

No one is permitted to accept more Mass stipends to be cele-

---

265. c. 828.
266. It is certain that there is a serious obligation to satisfy the entire number of stipends; it is commonly taught that in every case there is a serious obligation of restitution no matter how small the stipend. Some hold that the omission of one Mass in a large number (e.g., 100) for the same intention, or when an unsatisfied stipend is extremely low (e.g., ten cents), the obligation of restitution is probably not serious.
267. c. 829. It is otherwise when the stipends have not been accepted or received.
268. c. 830. Often in some places, as in large cities, the usual stipend is larger than the diocesan norm; thus a donor in such places is to be considered to give that stipend.
269. S.C. Conc. 15 iun. 1928.

brated by himself than he can satisfy within a year.[270] This does not bind if the donor explicitly states that the Masses could be celebrated at any time even beyond the expiration of a year; the same is implicitly indicated when the donor requests more Masses than days in the year, e.g., 400. The limitation of one year does not affect the priest, if in accepting the stipends it is understood that he will send them to another priest or priests. In churches which, because of the special devotion of the faithful, there is such an abundance of Mass stipends that all the Masses cannot be celebrated there in due time, the faithful should be informed by a notice posted in an accessible and frequented place that the Masses requested will be celebrated either there, when it is convenient to do so, or elsewhere.[271]

6. *Time Specified for Celebration*

Masses for the celebration of which a time has been expressly specified by the donor must be celebrated exactly at that time.[272] The time is expressly, although implicitly, specified if the stipend is offered for success in a scholastic examination or in some endeavor or for the happy death of a dying person, etc. The obligation to observe the time specified obliges under serious sin, if it is a necessary (*sine qua non*) condition (and also restitution obliges). If the donor did not so express himself, manual Masses requested for an urgent purpose must be celebrated as soon as possible relative to the purpose to be attained (*tempus utile*)[273] i.e., before the realization of the purpose for which the Mass was requested becomes useless or impossible. In other cases the Masses are to be celebrated within a short time considering the larger or smaller number of Masses requested.[274]

270. c. 835.
271. c. 836.
272. c. 834, 1.
273. Ibid., 2, 1o.
274. **Ibid.,** 2o. The decree **"Ut debita"** of the S.C. Conc. (11 maii 1904) still serves as the norm of reference and recommendation for commentators, although it is no longer preceptive; according to its terms the **"intra modicum tempus"** of the canon is to be understood as one month for one Mass, six months for one hundred Masses, and one year for all the

If the donor should expressly leave to the priest the determination of the time of celebration of the masses, he may celebrate them at the time most convenient for him.[275] It is usually recommended in practice that Masses be said as soon as convenient and in the order of their reception, unless certain ones must be said sooner.

7. *Place of Celebration*

It is presumed that the donor wishes only the application of the Mass; if, however, he expressly specified certain circumstances to be observed in the celebration of Mass, the priest who accepted the stipend must carry out his intention.[276] Unless a particular place was stipulated for the celebration as a necessary (*sine qua non*) condition, there is no obligation to return the stipend if this circumstance is not observed. Usually such an omission is not seriously culpable and is even excused by a reasonable cause. If there is an obligation to celebrate on a privileged altar, the obligation is not satisfied by offering Mass elsewhere or by the application of another plenary indulgence. To rectify an error made in good faith, the safer course in practice is to apply another Mass on a privileged altar.[277]

8. *Other Qualifications*

It is commonly taught that failure to observe the circumstances requested by the donor does not exceed a slight sin, in the absence

Masses received, with other numbers computed in proportion, and all reckoned morally and not mathematically. This implies that the Masses have been given to the same priest by one and the same donor; if the donors are all different persons, each has its own computation, e.g., thirty stipends, each of which is from a different offerer, should be satisfied in a month (S.C. Conc. 27 feb. 1905).

---

275. **Ibid.,** 3o, i.e., as long as it is within the year from their reception (c. 835). A delay beyond the "**modicum tempus**" is sinful; it is certainly a serious sin if Masses are delayed beyond the year (prescinding from a circumstance determining their exact time), probably a slight sin if the delay is notably beyond the above norm, except with a just and reasonable cause.
276. c. 833.
277. Cf. S.C. Indulg. 22 feb. 1847; 2 maii 1852; 24 iul, 1885.

of a reasonable cause, unless the circumstance was necessarily attached (*sine qua non*), and then the stipend must be restored. Unless express agreement was made for one or the other, a Mass for the deceased is satisfied by the celebration of any Mass, and a Requiem Mass may be celebrated for the living.[278] The circumstance of a sung Mass, a privileged altar, a Gregorian series, etc., however, must be observed. If a sung Mass was requested, a recited Mass will be valid, but at least a sung Mass must be celebrated later without being applied for the intention of the original donor. If no offering is made for a nuptial Mass or a funeral Mass, it is not strictly necessary to offer the Mass for the couple or for the deceased, and the celebrant may satisfy another stipend obligation,[279] but it is most fitting to apply the Masses, especially in the case of the poor.[280] There is no obligation on the part of the priest accepting a stipend to celebrate the Mass personally; he may transfer it to another priest. Even if the donor indicates a desire for the recipient of the stipend to say the Mass, failure to do so rarely becomes a serious sin.

Gregorian Masses are a set of thirty Masses celebrated at any altar for thirty consecutive days for the soul of one departed. It is piously believed that these Masses or Trental have a special efficacy for liberating souls from Purgatory through the intercession of St. Gregory the Great; the Church has approved the practice but never enriched it with any indulgence.[281] There is a serious obligation to celebrate the series of Gregorian Masses on thirty consecutive days. The series must be offered for a deceased person,[282] and for only one person,[283] although the daily Mass need not be a Requiem

278. Cf. **ibid.,** 11 apr. 1840; S.C. Conc. 27 apr. 1895.
279. Cf. S. Off. 1 sept. 1841; S.C. Conc. 27 apr. 1895.
280. Cf. c. 1235.
281. S.C. Indulg. 11 mart 1884: "The confidence by which the faithful retain the celebration of the Gregorian thirty Masses (i.e., lead by the example of St. Gregory the Great) as especially efficacious by the good will and acceptance of the divine mercy for the liberation of a soul from the pains of Purgatory, is pious and reasonable, and the custom of celebrating these Masses is approved by the Church."
282. **Ibid.,** 24 aug. 1888.
283. **Ibid.,** 14 ian. 1889.

Mass,[284] and the same priest need not say the series. The series is not considered to be interrupted by the last three days of Holy Week[285] and one Mass on Christmas in connection with the series suffices. The series should be renewed if it is broken culpably.

If the series should be interrupted because of an unforeseen impediment (e.g., illness) or some other reasonable cause (e.g., a funeral or wedding Mass) the benefits or fruits of the suffrage which the practice of the Church and the piety of the faithful have heretofore recognized, are preserved by the disposition of the Church, with the obligation still binding of the priest celebrant to complete the thirty Masses as soon as possible.[286]

9. Consignment or Transference of Stipends

He who has a number of Masses which he is allowed to give to others may distribute them among priests of his choice, provided he knows that they are trustworthy or are recommended by the testimony of their Ordinary.[287] This is with respect to manual stipends only and the local Ordinary may not forbid their transference outside the diocese. He who has Masses to be celebrated by others is to distribute them as soon as possible, but the lawful time for their celebration begins with the day of their reception by the priest undertaking the obligation, unless there is some other provision made.[288] Administrators of pious causes and executors of wills and bequests are bound to this early or undelayed transference. He who has given to other priests Masses which he has received from the faithful, or which are in any way entrusted to him, is held to their obligation until he receives notice that the stipends have been received by the priest-transferee and that he has accepted the obligation.[289] This notice may be given orally or in writing and is implied in a personal hand to hand transferal. A postal money

284. S. Off. 12 dec. 1912.
285. S.C. Conc. 7 maii 1791.
286. S.C. Conc. 24 feb. 1967.
287. c. 838. S.C.E.O., 7 ian. 1930, requires that all stipends for Oriental priests outside their own territory be sent to the Oriental Congregation or the Apostolic Delegate.
288. c. 837.
289. c. 839.

order receipt or a cancelled check is not necessarily indicative that the consignee himself has received the stipend money or that he accepts the obligations. Until the stipends are accepted, any loss of them, even without fault, is the responsibility of the consignor and thus he is obliged to make good on the Mass obligations.[290]

One who sends to others manual stipends for Masses is to send the entire sum received, unless the donor has expressly permitted a portion of the stipend to be retained or it is clearly established that the portion in excess of the diocesan stipend was given for the benefit of the immediate recipient (*intuitu personae*).[291] It is more commonly held that to retain a portion of a stipend outside the cases permitted by law is a serious violation of commutative justice and binds seriously to restitution. Title to a stipend is conditioned on the celebration of the Mass; thus this title passes to the actual celebrant when the stipend is transferred and the consignor consequently retains no just claim to any portion. Expenses of transferal and administration of stipends may be deducted but the sonsignor may not lawfully profit in an exchange rate transaction in such way that the entire stipend is not transferred. Moreover, he cannot satisfy his obligation of celebrating Mass for a stipend through another priest to whom he has given a smaller stipend.[292] Expenses involved in finding a priest to celebrate novena Masses for which rather generous stipends have been offered cannot be deducted from the stipends owing to the celebrant.[293] A pastor who commits another priest to say a funeral or nuptial Mass is bound to give the celebrant the usual stipend for the Mass (recited or sung) for that hour and may retain the remainder of the offering as the stole fee.[294]

Unless the intention of the founder provides otherwise, the excess for Masses *ad instar manualium* is lawfully retained, and

290. Cf. c. 829.
291. c. 840, 1. Penalties may be incurred for violations of the laws on Mass stipends (c. 2324).
292. S. Off. 24 sept. 1665. Benedict XIV, 3 iun. 1741 stated that it was a detestable abuse for the priest transmitting a stipend to ask the celebrant to let him keep a portion of the stipend.
293. S.C. Conc. 16 apr. 1921.
294. Cf. **ibid.,** 28 mart., 25 iul., 22 aug. 1874; 10 nov. 1917.

it is sufficient to remit only the manual alms of the diocese where
the Mass is celebrated if the larger stipend takes the place of the
partial endowment of the benefit or pious cause.[295] Without exception all administrators of pious causes as well as all who in any
way are bound to the fulfillment of Mass obligations, whether they
are clerics or laymen, are, at the end of each year, to send to their
Ordinaries in the manner which the latter specify all yet unsatisfied
Mass obligations.[296] Constitutions of religious institutes may make
further regulations.

10. *Record and Surveillance of Stipends*

Rectors of churches and other pious places, secular and religious,
in which it is customary to receive stipends, are to have a special
book in which they accurately record the number of stipends received, the intention for which they are given, the amount of the
stipend, and the fact of the celebration of the Mass.[297] At least
once a year Ordinaries are obliged to inspect books of this kind
in person or through others.[298] Local Ordinaries and religious superiors who entrust the celebration of Masses to their own subjects
or to others are to record promptly in a book in the proper order
the stipends they have received together with their amount, and
they are to exert every effort to see that the Masses are celebrated as
soon as possible.[299] All priests, secular and religious, must accurately record the intentions they have received and the fact of having
satisfied them.[300] This is a serious obligation; in the event of the
incapacity or death of the priest unsatisfied Mass obligations are
more easily perceived and taken care of.

295. c. 840, 2.
296. c. 841, 1. S.C. Conc. 19 feb. 1921 holds that funded Masses,
     those **ad instar manualium** and manual Masses given for the
     benefit of a pious cause are subject to the direction of the
     Ordinary.
297. c. 843, 1. Religious constitutions may impose this duty on the
     sacristan or someone else.
298. **Ibid.,** 2.
299. c. 844, 1. Masses are generally to be transferred in their order
     of reception.
300. **Ibid.,** 2. Those in charge of a church seem to have no obliga-
     tion to keep the record after the Masses have been said.

The right and obligation of seeing that the Mass obligations are satisfied belongs in churches of seculars to the local Ordinary and in those of religious to the superior.[301]

Every semblance of trading or selling must be entirely removed from Mass stipends.[302] The practice is tolerated where pastors defray the expenses of boarding and lodging assistants from Mass stipends received from Masses celebrated by the latter, provided that the pastor makes no profit from the practice and provided that the Ordinary is alert to prevent any abuse.[303] The pooling of Mass stipends in parishes is tolerated and is not unlawful, as long as all the priests involved give their consent. Profit is not sought thereby and the incidental increase accruing to a given priest is freely renounced by the others. The arrangement cannot be imposed by the pastor upon his assistant, and those not participating in it are not entitled to a share of the fund.

11. *Translation, Condonation, and Reduction of Mass Obligations*

The faculty of transferring Masses which should be offered in a particular place or at a specified time to another place or time may be granted by the Holy See, usually because of the scarcity of

301. c. 842. The right and obligation of inspection in parish churches entrusted to exempt religious belong to the religious superior (S.C. Ep. et Reg. 11 maii 1940).
302. c. 827. It is forbidden for publishers to collect stipends and have the Masses celebrated by priests who would then accept books instead of the money and permit the publishers to profit by a commission on the stipends and the books or to receive the usual profit on the books, so that however the operation is accomplished, a profit accrues to anyone but the celebrant of the Mass (S.C. Conc. 11 maii 1904). This differs from the priest receiving wine, oil, grain, poultry, etc., as an offering. Religious, for example, may make an agreement to assume the celebration of certain Masses and the stipends for the same to be retained by the other religious in the agreement, in order to defray certain expenses or obligations owed to the other parties, e.g., taxes, liturgical books., etc.
303. S.C. Conc. 27 feb. 1905; 11 ian. 1920.

priests. Limited power in this area is granted local Ordinaries in the U.S.A. by quinquennial faculties.

Condonation is the forgiveness granted by competent authority for the *past* omission of Masses, either manual or funded, which should have been celebrated but were not. The Holy Father alone has the power of condonation, which he may exercise for a just and proportionate cause, supplying for the defect from the treasury of the Church.

Reduction is the lessening or reducing of the number of Masses *to be said*, which may be granted by the Holy See for a just cause. The donors of the stipends suffer no damage, since the deficiency is supplied from the spiritual treasury of the Church. Local Ordinaries have the faculty[304] to reduce, because of diminished revenue and for as long as the situation endures, perpetual legacy Masses to the measure of the stipend legitimately in vogue in the diocese, provided there is no one who is bound and who can be practically compelled to increase the stipend. They likewise have the faculty to reduce obligations or legacies of Masses binding on benefices or other ecclesiastical institutions if the returns from the benefice or institution prove insufficient for the adequate support of the beneficiary and for the discharge of the sacred ministries, if any are attached to the benefice, or for the suitable accomplishment of the purpose proper to the said ecclesiastical institution.

Until further notice, Pope Paul VI has reserved to himself[305] the entire question of reducing, condoning, and commuting the obligations of Masses. From February 1, 1972 all general and special faculties previously granted at any time, for any cause, and to any physical or moral person, by force of law or by the pope or his predecessors, directly, orally, or through the sacred dicasteries, are suspended, with the exception of the faculties granted the local Ordinaries in numbers 11-12 of the *motu proprio Pastorale Munus*.

---

304. Motu proprio **Pastorale munus,** 11-12. These faculties permit Bishops to reduce, but not to exstinguish, the obligation of funded Masses which has culpably in the past not been satisfied, bearing in mind as far as possible the will of the founders or offerers (Pont. Com. Decretis Conc. Vat. II Interp., resp. I, 1 iul. 1971).

305. Sec. Status, 29 nov. 1971.

Appendix

Instruction *Immensae Caritatis* on Facilitating Sacramental Communion in Particular Circumstances

Christ the Lord has left to the Church, his Spouse, a testament of his immense love. This wonderful gift of the Eucharist, which is the greatest gift of all, demands that such an important mystery should be increasingly better known and its saving power more fully shared. With the intention of fostering devotion to the Eucharist —the summit and center of Christian worship—the Church, moved by pastoral zeal and concern, has on more than one occasion issued suitable laws and appropriate documents.

Present-day conditions however demand that, while the utmost reverence owing to such a Sacrament[1] is constantly maintained,

---

1. Cf. Council of Trent, Session 13, **Decretum de SS. Eucharistiae Sacramento,** c. 7; D.880(1646-1647): "If it is not fitting for any-one to approach any sacred functions except in a state of holiness, then certainly to the extent that the holiness and godli-ness of this heavenly Sacrament is more and more known to the Christian, all the more must he take care that he does not come to receive it without great reverence and holiness, espe-cially because of the fearful words of the Apostle which we read: 'A person who eats and drinks without recognizing the Body of the Lord is eating and drinking his own condemnation' (1 Cor 11:29). Thus the following precept should be recalled to the one desirous of receiving Holy Communion: 'Let a man so examine himself' (1 Cor 11:28). Ecclesiastical custom de-clares that the proving of one's self is necessary, so that no one, conscious of having committed mortal sin, though considering himself contrite, should approach the Holy Eucharist without first having made a sacramental confession. This holy Synod declares that this must perpetually be observed by all Christians, even by priests, whose duty it is to celebrate Mass, as long as there is an availability of confessors. If in the case of urgent necessity a priest will have celebrated without previous con-fession, he is to make a confession as soon as possible." Sacred Congregation of the Council, Decree **Sacra Tridentina Synodus,** (20 December 1905): **ASS** 38 (1905-1906), pp. 400-406; Sacred Con-gregation for the Doctrine of the Faith, **Normae pastorales circa absolutionem sacramentalem generali modo impertiendam** (31 July 1972), Norm 1: **AAS** 64, (1972), p. 511.

greater access to Holy Communion should be made possible so that the faithful, by sharing more fully in the fruits of the sacrifice of the Mass, might dedicate themselves more readily and effectively to God and to the good of the Church and of mankind.

First of all provision must be made lest reception become impossible or difficult owing to a lack of a sufficient number of ministers. Provision must also be made lest the sick be deprived of such a great spiritual consolation by being impeded from receiving Holy Communion because of the law of fast, which they may not be able to observe, even though it be already very moderate. Finally, it seems appropriate to determine in which circumstances the faithful who ask to receive sacramental Communion a second time on the same day may be permitted fittingly to do so.

After a study of the recommendations of certain episcopal conferences the following norms are issued in regard to:

1. extraordinary ministers for the distribution of Holy Communion;
2. a more extensive faculty of receiving Holy Communion twice in the same day;
3. mitigation of the Eucharistic fast for the sick and elderly;
4. the piety and reverence owing to the Blessed Sacrament whenever the Eucharist is placed in the hand of the communicant.

1

EXTRAORDINARY MINISTERS FOR THE DISTRIBUTION OF HOLY COMMUNION

There are various circumstances in which a lack of sufficient ministers for the distribution of Holy Communion can occur:

during Mass, because of the size of the congregation or a particular difficulty in which a celebrant finds himself;

outside of Mass, when it is difficult because of distance to take the sacred species, especially the Viaticum, to the sick in danger of death, or when the very number of the sick, especially in hospitals and similar institutions, requires many ministers. Therefore, in order that the faithful, who are in the state of grace and who with an upright and pious disposition, wish to share in the Sacred Banquet, may not be deprived of this sacramental help and consolation, it has seemed appropriate to the Holy Father to establish extraordinary ministers, who may give Holy Communion to themselves and to other faithful under the following determined conditions:

I Local Ordinaries have the faculty to permit a suitable person individually chosen as an extraordinary minister for a specific occasion or for a time or, in the case of necessity, in some permanent way, either to give the Eucharist to himself or to other faithful and to take it to the sick who are confined to their homes. This faculty may be used whenever:

a) there is no priest, deacon or acolyte;
b) these are prevented from administering Holy Communion because of another pastoral ministry or because of ill health or advanced age;
c) the number of faithful requesting Holy Communion is such that the celebration of Mass or the distribution of the Eucharist outside of Mass would be unduly prolonged.

II Local Ordinaries also have the faculty to permit individual priests exercising their sacred office to appoint a suitable person who in cases of genuine necessity would distribute Holy Communion for a specific occasion.

III The above-mentioned Local Ordinaries can delegate these faculties to auxiliary bishops, episcopal vicars and episcopal delegates.

IV The suitable person to whom numbers I and II refer shall be designated according to the following order: lector, student of major seminary, male religious, woman religious, catechist, Catholic man or woman. This order however can be changed according to the prudent judgment of the Local Ordinary.

V In oratories of religious communities of either sex the office of distributing Holy Communion in the circumstances described in number I can fittingly be given to a male superior not having major orders or to a woman superior or to their respective vicars.

VI If time permits, it is fitting that the suitable person individually chosen by the Local Ordinary for administering Holy Communion, as well as the person appointed by a priest having the faculty spoken of in number II, should receive the mandate according to the rite annexed to this Instruction; they are to distribute Holy Communion according to the liturgical norms.

Since these faculties are granted only for the spiritual good of the faithful and for cases of genuine necessity, priests are to remember that they are not thereby excused from the task of distributing the Eucharist to the faithful who legitimately request it, and especially from taking and giving it to the sick.

The person who has been appointed to be an extraordinary minister of Holy Communion is necessarily to be duly instructed and should distinguish himself by his Christian life, faith and morals. Let him strive to be worthy of this great office; let him cultivate devotion to the Holy Eucharist and show himself as an example to the other faithful by his piety and reverence for this most holy Sacrament of the altar. Let no one be chosen whose selection may cause scandal among the faithful.

2

THE EXTENDED FACULTY FOR RECEIVING HOLY COMMUNION TWICE IN THE SAME DAY

According to the discipline currently in force, the faithful are permitted to receive Holy Communion a second time:

on the evening of Saturday or of the day preceding a holyday of obligation, when they intend to fufil the precept of hearing Mass, even though they have already received Holy Communion in the morning of that same day:[2]

at the second Mass of Easter and at one of the Masses celebrated on Christmas Day, even if they have already received Holy Communion at the Mass of the Paschal Vigil or at the midnight Mass of Christmas:[3]

likewise at the evening Mass of Holy Thursday, even if they have received Holy Communion at the earlier Mass of the Chrism.[4]

Since, beyond these circumstances which have been mentioned, there are similar occasions which suggest that Holy Communion might fittingly be received twice in the same day, it is necessary here to determine more precisely the reasons for the new faculty.

The norm which the Church, a most provident Mother, has introduced according to venerable custom and included in canon law by which the faithful are permitted to receive Holy Communion only once a day remains intact nor it it permitted to be set aside merely from motives of devotion. To a simple desire for repeated reception of Holy Communion it should be answered that the power of the Sacrament by which faith, charity and the other virtues are nourished, strengthened and expressed is all the greater to the extent that one more devoutly approaches the sacred table.[5] For, from the liturgical celebration the faithful should go out to the works of charity, piety and apostolic action so that "they may hold fast by their conduct and life to what they have received by faith and the Sacrament."[6]

2. Sacred Congregation of Rites, Instruction **Eucharisticum Mysterium** (25 May 1967), 28; **AAS** 59 (1967), p. 557.
3. Cf. **Ibid.**
4. Cf. **Ibid.**; Sacred Congregation of Rites, Instruction **Inter Oecumenici** (26 September 1964), 60: **AAS** 56 (1964), p. 891; Instruction, **Tres abhinc annos** (4 May 1967), 14: **AAS** 59 (1967), p. 445.
5. Cf. S. Thomas, **Summa Theol.** III, q. 79, a. 7 ad 3 and a. 8 ad 1.
6. Sacred Congregation of Rites, Instruction **Eucharisticum Mysterium** (25 May 1967), 13: **AAS** 59 (1967), p. 549.

Special circumstances however can occur when the faithful who have already received Holy Communion that same day, or even priests who have already celebrated Mass, may be present at some community celebration. They may receive Holy Communion again in the following instances:

1. at those Masses in which the Sacraments of Baptism, Confirmation, Anointing of the Sick, Sacred Orders and Matrimony are administered; also at a Mass at which First Communion is received;[7]

2. at Masses at which a church or altar is consecrated; at Masses of religious profession or for the conferring of a 'canonical mission';

3. at the following Masses of the Dead: the funeral Mass, the Mass celebrated after notification of death, the Mass on the day of final burial and the Mass on the first anniversary;

4. at the principal Mass celebrated in the cathedral or in the parish on the feast of Corpus Christi and on the day of a parochial visitation; at the Mass celebrated by the major superior of a religious community on the occasion of a canonical visitation, of special meetings or chapters;

5. at the principal Mass of a Eucharistic or Marian Congress, whether international or national, regional or diocesan;

6. at the principal Mass of any congress, sacred pilgrimage or preaching mission for the people;

7. in the administration of Viaticum, in which Communion can also be given to the relatives and friends of the patient;

8. Also, Local Ordinaries may, besides those cases mentioned above, grant permission "ad actum" to receive Holy Communion twice in the same day, as often as they shall judge it truly justified by reason of genuinely special circumstances, according to the norm of this Instruction.

---

7. Cf. **Missale Romanum, Institutio generalis Missalis Romani,** 329 a, typical edition 1970, p. 90.

3

MITIGATION OF THE EUCHARISTIC FAST FOR THE SICK AND THE AGED

Above all it remains firmly decreed that a person to whom Viaticum is administered in danger of death is not bound by any law of fasting.[8] Likewise remaining in force is the concession already granted by Pius XII whereby "the sick, even if not confined to bed, can take non-alcoholic drinks and medicines in either liquid or solid form before the celebration of Mass and the reception of the Eucharist without any restriction of time."[9]

In the case of foods and drinks taken for the purpose of nutrition that tradition is to be respected according to which the Eucharist should be received, as Tertullian said, "before any food"[10] so as to indicate the excellence of the sacramental food.

In order to appreciate the dignity of the Sacrament and to prepare with joy for the coming of the Lord, a time of silence and recollection before the reception of Holy Communion is opportune. In the case of the sick, however, it will be a sufficient sign of piety and reverence if, for a brief period of time, they turn their minds to the greatness of the mystery. The period of time of the Eucharistic fast or abstinence from food and alcoholic drink is reduced to approximately one quarter of an hour, for the following:

1. the sick in hospitals or in their own homes, even if they are not confined to bed;

2. the faithful advanced in age who must remain at home because of age or who are living in a home for the aged;

3. sick priests, even if not confined to bed, and elderly priests, who wish to celebrate Mass or receive Holy Communion;

8. Cf. CIC 858, paragraph 1.
9. Motu Proprio, **Sacrum Communionem** (19 March 1957), 4; **AAS** 49 (1957), p. 178.
10. **Ad uxorem** 2,5: **PL** 1, 1408.

4. persons looking after the sick and the aged as well as those relatives of the sick and aged wishing to receive Holy Communion with them, whenever they are unable to observe the fast of one hour without inconvenience.

4

PIETY AND REVERENCE TOWARDS THE BLESSED SACRAMENT, WHEN THE EUCHARIST IS PLACED IN THE HANDS OF THE FAITHFUL

Since the Instruction *Memoriale Domini* was published three years ago, some episcopal conferences have sought the faculty from the Apostolic See to allow the minister of Holy Communion to place the Eucharistic species in the hands of the faithful. As that Instruction recalled, "the precepts of the Church and the documents of the Fathers amply testify that the deepest reverence and the greatest prudence have been shown with regard to the Holy Eucharist,"[11] and should continue to be shown. Especially in this manner of receiving Holy Communion some points indicated by experience should be most carefully observed.

Let the greatest diligence and care be taken particularly with regard to fragments which perhaps break off the hosts. This applies to the minister and to the recipient whenever the Sacred Host is placed in the hands of the communicant.

Before initiating the practice of giving Holy Communion in the hand a suitable instruction and catechesis of Catholic doctrine is necessary concerning both the real and permanent presence of Christ under the Eucharistic species and the reverence due to this Sacrament.[12] It is necessary to instruct the faithful that Jesus Christ is the Lord and Saviour and that the same worship and adoration

---

11. Sacred Congregation for Divine Worship, Instruction **Memoriale Domini** (29 May 1969); **AAS** 61 (1969), p. 542.
12. Cf. Second Vatican Council, Constitution on the Sacred Liturgy, **Sacrosanctum Concilium**, 7: **AAS** 56 (1969), pp. 100-101; Sacred Congregation of Rites, Instruction **Eucharisticum Mysterium** (25 May 1967), 9: **AAS** 59 (1967), p. 547.

given to God is owed to him present under the sacramental signs. Let the faithful be counselled therefore not to omit a sincere and fitting thanksgiving after the Eucharistic banquet, such as may accord with each one's particular ability, state and duties.[13] So that participation in this heavenly table may be altogether worthy and profitable, the value and effects deriving from it for both the individual and the community must be pointed out to the faithful in such a way that their familiar attitude reveals reverence, fosters that intimate love for the Father of the household who gives us "our daily bread"[14] and leads to a living relationship with Christ of whose flesh and blood we partake.[15]

The Supreme Pontiff Paul VI has approved and sanctioned this Instruction by his authority, and directed that it should be published, decreeing that it should enter into force on the day of its publication.

Given in Rome, at the Sacred Congregation for the Discipline of the Sacraments, 29 January 1973.

A. Card. Samoré, Prefect

✠ J. Casoria, Secretary

13. Paul VI, Address **Ad Membra Consilii Eucharisticis ex omnibus Nationibus conventibus moderandis habita: AAS** 64 (1972), p. 287.
14. Cf. Lk 11:3.
15. Cf. Heb 2:14.